MW01633239

Books by Kenneth Koch

POETRY

Poems
Ko, or A Season on Earth
Permanently
Thank You and Other Poems
When the Sun Tries to Go On
The Pleasures of Peace
The Art of Love
The Duplications
The Burning Mystery of Anna in 1951
Days and Nights
Selected Poems: 1950–1982
On the Edge
Seasons on Earth

FICTION

Interlocking Lives
The Red Robins

THEATER

Bertha and Other Plays
A Change of Hearts
The Red Robins

EDUCATIONAL WORKS

Wishes, Lies, and Dreams:
    Teaching Children to Write Poetry
Rose, Where Did You Get That Red?:
    Teaching Great Poetry to Children
I Never Told Anybody:
    Teaching Poetry Writing in a Nursing Home
Sleeping on the Wing:
    An Anthology of Modern Poetry (WITH KATE FARRELL)

ONE
THOUSAND
AVANT-GARDE
PLAYS

KENNETH KOCH

Alfred A. Knopf   New York   1988

ONE THOUSAND AVANT-GARDE PLAYS

THIS IS A BORZOI BOOK
PUBLISHED BY ALFRED A. KNOPF, INC.

Many of the poems in this volume appeared in slightly different form in *Artforum, Boulevard, Grand Street, New American Writing, Poetry Project Newsletter,* and the East Hampton *Star.*

Library of Congress Cataloging-in-Publication Data

Koch, Kenneth.
    One thousand avant-garde plays.

    One hundred twelve of the author's plays.
      I. Title.   II. Title: 1000 avant-garde plays.
PS3521.027054 1988   812'.54   87-46074
ISBN 0-394-56925-3
ISBN 0-394-75897-8 (pbk.)

Manufactured in the United States of America
First Edition

To Charity

Acknowledgments

For help and inspiration of various kinds, I thank Charity Gardner, Kate Farrell, Anne Porter, Barbara Vann, David Hollister, and Donald Sanders. I am particularly indebted to the great French historian Fernand Braudel, in whose books, especially *The Mediterranean World* and *The Structures of Everyday Life*, I found the ideas for a number of these plays.

Here I am at the beginning of the first volume, and the most complicated of the three. Each chapter may not in itself seem difficult to the reader; but the complication is the insidious result of the large number of aims I have in mind, the painful uncovering of unusual themes which must all be incorporated into a coherent history. . . . Why try to bring them together?

FERNAND BRAUDEL
The Structures of Everyday Life

. . . [Mayakowsky] has a description of a trip from Sevastopol to Yalta.

A short trip, like life.

On the other side of the Baidar Gates, the sea reveals itself like unexpected love. Life is not the same. Without these clouds, without the bay, without this sea—each bit of which you love—it is utterly impossible to live.

VIKTOR SHKLOVSKY
Mayakowsky and His Circle

Contents

ONE
THOUSAND
AVANT-GARDE
PLAYS

Time and His Trumpet

(Enter TOMMY TIME, *with a trumpet. He plays one note, then stops.)*

TOMMY TIME
>Whenever I blow this horn, things change,
>And they are changing all the time
>This time I am taking out to talk to you
>Is no time, does not exist in time, you are not
>Changing, you are not growing older, your
>Love stays the same. It is
>A privileged moment. But when I start to blow
>It will be time, and you will be changing again!

MAN
>But my love stays the same.

TOMMY TIME
>That is because it is changing with time.

MAN
>It just stopped.

TOMMY TIME
>Because I stopped playing.

WOMAN
>Oh, play again!

MAN
>Play, Tommy Time! Without time I feel nothing.

WOMAN
>So that's what that noise was we heard all the time!

MAN
>The noise of change!

TOMMY TIME
>Or of FAITHFULNESS, which also lives in time.

Manet

(Paris, in the nineteenth century.)

MAN

What is the connection

WOMAN

Between the newly emerging modern democratic society

MAN

And the art of Edouard Manet?

WOMAN

Here. This book tells it.

(Time passes and society is altered: there are the sights and sounds of the twentieth century.)

BOTH

And now it has all gone away!

Elfred the Dancer

(Red and orange scarves and an atmosphere of all of history at the same time.)

ELFRED
> When maids become historians
> And summer skies change
> To violent thunder-rattling scarves or plates,
> Then Macedon at last yields to Greek influence
> And conquers while being conquered.
> Alexander did this.
> The story is told by his maid.
> Alexander had no maid.
> I am Elfred the Dancer.

Searching for Fairyland

(Mist.)

WILLIAM BUTLER YEATS
I have coom all this distance, lookin for faeryland.

OLD CRONE
Well, ye have time, auld father. Tis not yet dark.

WILLIAM BUTLER YEATS
Accents change, and all things change, but Beauty is like a stone.

(A snowfall.)

Tawai Nakimo

(The bare stage of Noh drama.)

TAWAI NAKIMO
I am Tawai Nakimo, famed beauty, courtesan of the Emperor Wai.

(dreamily, transported, for a moment, to the past)

How we dance to the slosh of silk and bracelets!

(returns to the present)

Now my age is ninety-seven,
And I have come to this bridge land to seek retreat.
How strange that, around me, all, all is bridges.
Bridge over river, bridge over stream,
Bridge over roadway; here, even, bridge over little girl.
Everything, it seem, here have it own bridge.

(in a sort of visionary ecstasy)

What is the bridge over me, bridge that passes above the head of
Tawai Nakimo?

Incident on the Street

8

(MAN comes up to another man, HARRIMAN, on the street and offers him a rather large box.)

MAN

    Harriman, I have brought you this box of balls—
    Wooden balls and steel balls, and balls with gold upon them,
    Acorn balls, nylon balls, balls of porphyry and of ancient silver,
    Every kind of ball you can imagine that is of human make.

(MAN leaves.)

The Brave Bull

MATADOR
> Toro! Toro!

(He makes the kill. From the fallen BULL *rises the* SPIRIT OF THE BULL.*)*

SPIRIT OF THE BULL
> I, who was once the body of the bull
> And am now its spirit, come near you.
> And, near you as I am, I shall take your life away.

MATADOR
> But my young sons and daughters!

SPIRIT OF THE BULL
> Never should a man have a family,
> Especially a large and growing family,
> When he knows he is going to be a bullfighter.
> I am sorry for this cruel and merciless act,
> But it has been fated
> By the white handkerchiefs, away!

(The SPIRIT *kills the* MATADOR. *Then the* SPIRIT *himself drops dead and is dragged around the ring.)*

SPECTATORS *(shouting in various languages)*
> Brave bull! Brave bull!

(Bullfight music.)

The Promenade in Oaxaca

(Evening. EDWARD *is in his forties;* CHRISTINE *is fifteen.)*

EDWARD
> Christine, let's walk
> Down this street

CHRISTINE
> I heard
> Last night
> At the circus
> Someone died
> Of I don't know what

EDWARD
> Electrocution?
> Dog bite? Broken spine?
> Falling from seat? Bench collapse?
> Snake bite? Rat bite?
> We must not go to see
> This circus—
> O Christine
> Just one night
> And yet not having one night
> Fifteen years old
> Mystical summer
> Good night—
> Oh, my clearest, best!

Six Tones

(Each of the following speeches—lines—is shouted by a different person.)

SOON THE RACE WILL END

WHICH HORSE WILL WIN?

I ENTER THE RACETRACK

A GRAVE EXPRESSION IS ON HER FACE

BUT SHE DOES NOT CALL HIM

HER AGGRIEVED WOMANHOOD

The Cowries

(A sandy stretch by the sea.)

EDMUNDSON

>For seven years I have been accumulating cowrie shells,
>Going from island to island, from coast to coast,
>And I have made my fortune. Now I must leave this place.
>Hola there, you, fellow! I want to buy your boat.
>I'll give you seven shells.

OGON, A NATIVE

>I don't understand "buy."

EDMUNDSON

>I'll give you these shells. You give me the boat.
>*(He shows* OGON *some cowries.)*

OGON *(decisively)*

>No, Trader. We are not fools. You try to trick us!
>My boat can fly over the water. These shells cannot do that!

*(*OGON *gets into his boat and paddles off.)*

EDMUNDSON

>Perhaps . . . he's right—and what I do is wrong.
>What this old fellow's said has made me think—I'll leave these
>>shells . . . and find some better way.

*(*EDMUNDSON *drops his cowries on the sand, and goes. Sound of the sea.)*

Two Tall Individuals

FIRST
> The difference between a moment of action and a whole play.

SECOND
> You have never known that.

The End of Comedy

JOE
> You should do a vaudeville revue!

BILL
> But there are no stand-up comics like Mighty Head any more!

(Enter MIGHTY HEAD.*)*

MIGHTY HEAD
> Give me a light, boys, for I wants to smoke.
> Hey bobareebob, fellas, how's about a little joke?

JOE
> Okay, Mighty Head, will you act in a play for us?

MIGHTY HEAD
> No, I'm too old for that and too famous for that—
> I'm just my whole life one big joke.
> Ain't that enough? *(He acts crazy.)* Ack ack ack ack!

BILL
> Yes, Mighty Head, that is enough. He's amazing!

Cook

(The city of Chengde, early evening. COOK, *a young woman, is dressed all in white cook's clothing, including a round cook's hat.)*

COOK
>I am the Cook, I am racing through the street
>Of Chengde, with my rice boat and in my apron
>All of white and in my cooking hat of white
>My broad my smiling peasant face
>Does cause alarm by winning charm
>To all the masculine cook around
>I DON'T think
>
>Because this is China, land of think
>To work and always busy
>Cook who runs around shall find
>A young fellow to her mind
>When comes time
>For this. Meanwhile
>With cook-run-around, NO FLIRTING!!
>
>And no go to the paper store
>Until start of tomorrow day.
>And no go to the wedding store
>Cook shall not go away.
>Cook run through town. I am running!
>No one sees me. In despair
>None doth feel that I am fair.
>Cook running through town
>In no way this day holiday!

BRAD GARKS
>In U.S.A., my country, we have holiday parts in every day of the
>>year.
>Vast urban agglomerations spell out
>"I love you's" to dead green parks. O faithful Cook,
>Into my arms, now haste!

COOK

> You will not like me
> Because I am too much atmosphere of "Cook"
> And not woman-lady. Blad, good-bye!

Four Loves

Scene 1. A city street at night in spring.

SAM
Let's take a walk

MARINA
In the city

SAM
Till our shoes get wet

MARINA
It's been raining
All night.

SAM
Let's make music

(He plays a mandolin.)

I know you tonight
As I have never known

(Light shows a wall behind them that is all white stones.)

A book of white stones
Or symbolism

MARINA
Let's take a walk

SAM
If I kiss you please
Remember with your shoes off
You're so beautiful like
A lifted umbrella orange
And white

MARINA

Let's walk
Into the first
Rivers of morning

SAM

As you are seen
To be bathed in a light white light—
Come on

(They walk into such a light.)

Scene 2. A sidewalk and a big white door.

GIRL *(in pink)*

Good-bye. I'm leaving.

MAN *(in white)*

But this is only a sketch.

GIRL

Good-bye. I'm leaving.

MAN

But this is only a sketch.

GIRL

I'm leaving. Now. Good-bye.

(She leaves.)

Scene 3. A classroom.

MARY-JO PROFESSOR

Love comes into prominence as a theme
Earlier, sometimes, than the eighteenth century;
But, there, it dominates, overwhelms, pulverizes,
It is the theme of everything, the tema sine qua non.
No Smoking. No Gambling. No Eating. Make Way for Love.
It is the vrai Départ pour le Cythère.

*(EDMUNDSON *comes into the classroom, obviously smitten.)*

18

EDMUNDSON
Mary-Jo—I . . . I . . . I . . . I . . .

MARY-JO
Yes. But, please, the class must go on.

Scene 4. A street, near a small river.

SAM AT 20
Marina, I love you.

MARINA AT 20
Think about it again.

SAM AT 30
Now I am thirty years old.

MARINA AT 30
Think of it again.

SAM AT 40
I am forty years old.

MARINA AT 40
Think of me. Do you love me?

SAM AT 50
Now I am fifty. Marina!
Marina! I can't find you!
Why did you make me wait so long to decide?

(MARINA at 20, *heartbreakingly beautiful, goes past him in a boat on the river, guided by a* SWAN.)

MARINA AT 20
I guess I thought
We'd live forever and that it would always be the same!

The Umbrella of Stage Directions

(The Throne Room in Beijing.)

JAI FU, THE TRICKSTER
> In Hei-Nan we have something
> Called "The umbrella of stage directions."

KING
> What is it?

JAI FU
> You open this umbrella, and all stage directions come out.

KING
> What this means? I do can no in no way understand it—
> By the broad high streets of Beijing!

JAI FU
> Right this second, King,
> Umbrella is being opened outside
> And soon we will see—

(Big banging sound of umbrella snapping open with wind. Next, entering and exiting with astonishing rapidity, all kinds of characters, the STAGE DIREC-TIONS, *who fall down, laugh, weep, get up, fly about, open drawers, tear up pieces of paper, wring their hands, stomp, leap, go down on one knee, etc.)*

KING
> Ah! So beautiful!
> And how do stage directions end?

JAI FU
> Like this!

*(*JAI FU *signals to certain* STAGE DIRECTIONS, *who seize and bind, and gag, the* KING *and carry him off.* KING *re-enters, unbound and free.)*

KING

Oof! Very good. Clever. Now, you tell me:
These stage directions from many different plays?

(JAI FU *nods yes.*)

Let plays be brought in! I wish to
See them, *Minority Nationalities, Underground Army,
Blad Gark,* other ones. Keep here stage directions and
Bring plays.

STAGE DIRECTIONS

But we are part of plays, Majesty.

KING

No matter! Keep stage directions here!

JAI FU:

So shall it be!

(JAI FU *herds all* STAGE DIRECTIONS *to one side and encloses them in some kind
of fencing, from which they try, in vain, to escape.*)

The Party

AUTHOR *(at the door)*
>Is this the cast party?

HOST
>Yes. Who are you?

AUTHOR
>I'm the author.

HOST
>You can't come in!
>Good work follows bad work
>And good work follows good.
>Sometimes bad work follows bad.
>If you're the author you can't come in.

AUTHOR
>What about bad work following good?

HOST
>If you're the author you can't come in.

AUTHOR
>I only said I was the author.

HOST
>No one but the author would say that. No, go away! Good-bye!

(The door is closed.)

The Animated Room

(Characters sing lines operatically.)

MAN
Come back to me! Come back to me!

WOMAN
You didn't notice that I was the chair you were sitting on!

MAN
You didn't notice that I was the floor!

Happiness

(An atmosphere of Greek tragedy, specifically The Bacchae. *The god* HAPPI-NESS *is on a stark, sunny, dusty road entering a town. He carries a large sack.)*

HAPPINESS
>I am the God of Happiness and I am looking for twenty people to
>>make happy.
>But few can stand it. Few can support the happiness power that I
>>bring,
>It is too strong for most! I myself can barely transport it.
>Well. I will stop in this village, this town, this city, it is bigger
>Than I thought. Madame, where is the mayor or ruler or king of
>>this place?
>For I bring happiness. Your Ruler, once he has my precious gift,
>>can dispense it
>To others. But let him not give them too much,
>For it is dangerous—it is dangerous, and it can destroy!

*(*RULER *appears.)*

RULER
>I am the Ruler and I will take it.

*(*HAPPINESS *hands* RULER *the sack, "happiness," which consists of many small mirrors.* RULER *bends under its weight.)*

>Oh! I am staggering
>Dying under this horrible, beautiful weight!

HAPPINESS
>Give it to others
>Quickly! Unhappiness rides behind!

RULER
>I will! Ah! ah! Too late!
>Too much! Too strong!

(RULER *dies. The sack drops, the mirrors fall and break into many pieces.)*

TOWNSPEOPLE
Happiness! Happiness! We want some for ourselves!

(TOWNSPEOPLE *run out, pick up fragments of the glass, eat them, and die.)*

HAPPINESS
Disaster—again! Oh, misfortune.
Now to the next city I take my way.

(HAPPINESS *picks up his sack, which seems as full as ever, and goes away.)*

Searching for the Tomb of Alexander

(In the mountains of Crete. Fife music.)

EDWARD

> I am looking for the tomb of Alexander.

SHEPHERD

> To Macedon's wilds go, not here in Crete
> If you would find that doughty foe
> Who against all the world did go.

EDWARD

> I go
> In quest of Alexander.

The Tomb of Alexander

(A place in Macedon, with a tomb. ALEXANDER *is inside it.)*

ALEXANDER
 Inside here adamantly
 I sleep. I am trying to get out
 But can't.
 I am locked
 Inside the tomb of Alexander.

(Enter YOUNG MEN AND WOMEN *of Macedonia, singing gently but enthusiastically outside the tomb.)*

YOUNG MEN AND WOMEN
 Hey ho Alexander
 Gods bless Alexander
 He is great Alexander
 Alexander cinnamon tree!

An Atmosphere of Heavy, Intense (Summer) Stillness Pervades the World of Christine et Édouard

ÉDOUARD
>Let's sit down
>In this blazing garden,
>Christine.

CHRISTINE
>All right, Édouard. I can walk
>No more.
>I used to be fifteen
>But now I am sixteen
>And I am tired, so tired,
>After all.

ÉDOUARD
>Have we something to say?

(A silvery form, THE FUTURE, *makes a fleeting appearance.)*

CHRISTINE
>Yes, yes—Look! The Future!
>But now it's gone!

Mary Magdalene's Song

(The lines are spoken by PEOPLE *in the street, excitedly awaiting the appearance of* MARY MAGDALENE.*)*

Mary Magdalene's coming!

How can that be? She's long dead, in the Bible.

Nonetheless, she's coming along!
Get ready, to sing the bakery song!

Why does she like that one?

Who knows or can question
Mary Magdalene's tastes?
All we know is that she likes it
And that now she is coming along!

*(*MARY MAGDALENE *comes along, and the* PEOPLE *sing:)*

Bread and rolls
Fresh every day!
That's how we bake them,
The merry Magdalene way!

A Song to the Avant-Garde

TENOR

    In the beginning
The Avant-Garde
Was just a silly little thing,
Coconut-colored sidewalks,
Women with blue-white parasols
Tilting over backward
Or half backward—
In the beginning—
And then it grew, and became gigantic and hard
Like a great, great stone, the Avant-Garde—
Like a great, great stone that had usurped all of history!

CHORUS OF ÉMIGRÉ ARTISTS IN PARIS

    Oh, we'll walk down Apollinaire bis
Nine ninety nine
And construct back lugs
And clunk valentines
Of paired Z's
Ha ha ha ha, ha ha, hoo hoo
Ho Avant-Garde clear and light blue.

TENOR

    Everything went in fear of it,
Everyone walked in fear of it—
And yet it had no power, really,
It had no lasting power.
If now we celebrate it,
It is to salute it and to recognize it,
It is to urge it a little more to take the initiative,
Even though it might, by being so strange,
Destroy us! O Avant-Garde!
Come back, take heart, and tell us now
What life will, and what art will, do!

GHOSTLY VOICE *(offstage)*
    Maybe my mission is finished.
    Each movement in culture or history is but a stage
    Fitting to the age
    And it may be the one I had is ended.

TENOR
    Oh say not so, Avant-Garde!
    For those of us who have really loved you,
    Nothing, no one else can be as hard,
    And pure, and true.

GHOSTLY VOICE
    Well, then I'll try to be with you again!

(Great hullabaloo, wind, musical instruments, sounds of rending, tearing, crackling thunder, as of the Second Coming; and the AVANT-GARDE *appears— she is a small, old woman.)*

TENOR
    Avant-Garde! What's happened?

AVANT-GARDE
    This is but the initial phase!

(She waves a wand or stick, there is a crackle of blue and red lightning, and she is transformed into a shining, almost blinding CUBE.*)*

CUBE
    ANDIAM!

*(*CUBE *goes offstage triumphantly.)*

The Two Bulls

(The center of a bull ring, in Spain.)

FIRST BULL
Damn you! I wanted a bullfighter.

SECOND BULL
Well, what you have is another bull.

FIRST BULL
We circle each other, as in a dance.

SECOND BULL
Yes, but our intention is not to be graceful—

FIRST BULL
But somehow to seek an advantage—

SECOND BULL
Somehow to "win" by our mutual deaths.

(They charge each other. There are snorts, thuddings, and other bull-like noises.)

Spices

(An office in seventeenth-century Spain.)

FERNANDO DE PLAZA
>We need three tons of spice by Tuesday next.

ISAAC RUIZ
>Solomon Rosenstein is in Paris and can arrange the transfer
>Through Abraham Blum in Lisbon. Our cousin Izzy
>Barrasch will be waiting in Madrid
>For the order. Therefore you can count
>On having what you want within sixty days.

FERNANDO DE PLAZA
>But I need it by next Tuesday.

ISAAC RUIZ
>That possibility may come only after many years.
>This is the seventeenth century—

FERNANDO DE PLAZA
>Oh—but it—

ISAAC RUIZ
>At the beginning of Capitalism
>Which some say would not exist without the Jews
>And so you should be glad you are getting this order filled at all
>You should get down on your knees and thank God
>That you don't have to live in a feudal society forever
>Where everybody dies at age twelve and where you can't get
>>anything you want, ever,
>Unless it happens to be right next to you!

FERNANDO DE PLAZA
>I *am* grateful but don't like being grateful to you Jews!

ISAAC RUIZ
>Such is the lot that Heaven sends to both of us. L'chaim. Farewell!

(He goes. Sounds of heavy shipping.)

Happiness Comes Back, in a Car

*(*HAPPINESS *drives onstage in a small open car.)*

HAPPINESS

> If I come riding in a car, with the time, conceive me as a force, you
>> escaped from that theoretical
> Naturalism that has encapsulated you for so long.
> My destructiveness
> The playwright tries to control, but he cannot match it quite, it
> Overwhelms him. I can see
> Past and into your souls, you live too much without me
> Because you are afraid. I don't
> Blame you. I am Happiness
> Of a certain sort, that many will travel thousands of
> Miles to see. Then they try to manage to forget me
> And go about forgetful until they are old;
> Chancy it is if you can find me,
> Lucky if you can keep me for long.

(To a young couple on the street, ROB *and* PHILLIS.*)*

> You. Hello. Would you like to ride in my car?

PHILLIS

> Yes?

ROB

> All right.

*(*PHILLIS *and* ROB *get in the car, and* HAPPINESS *drives it off.* THREE PERSONS *on the sidewalk make comments.)*

FIRST

> Soon to be wed?

SECOND   Soon dead?

THIRD   Who knows?

Agamemnon

CURIOUS AND CONCERNED PERSON
    Aga
    Memnon

AGAMEMNON
    Yes—
    What?

CURIOUS AND CONCERNED PERSON
    In your
    Tomb is
    It hot?

AGAMEMNON
    I have
    Moved my
    Tomb to
    China
    Being
    There a-
    Mid the
    Classic Ming
    Frescoes, a
    Greek hotshot
    Travelers come
    From far away
    To see.

CURIOUS AND CONCERNED PERSON
    But isn't this a far
    Cry from being king?

AGAMEMNON
    It is, but when did I have anything
    That really made me happy? Murder and war.
    In death I feel I've found
    What Agamemnon was created for:

A world of Chinese ladies and
Long nights of love and laughter. And what's more—

CURIOUS AND CONCERNED PERSON
You're crazy, Agamemnon—

AGAMEMNON
Since I'm dead
What do you care what thoughts are in my head
Or how I dream away
The infinite night?

Husserl

(A Paris street. Two men, the philosopher HUSSERL *and a certain* JABOLINSKY, *are walking along in different-colored, enormous coats—perhaps one yellow, one red.)*

HUSSERL
>Well, Evelyn told me that her cape,
>The one she had at Longchamps do you remember, she said that
>>long blue lovely cape
>Had been torn to pieces by a cat. "Well, you know they have to
>>eat,"
>Said a philosopher; and I thought, "To hell with this! I'm
>Through being nice to him and to them, all of these
>>philosophers!"
>So I said, "Listen,
>I have Evelyn, I have a mental and spiritual home
>And I don't need you damned philosophers!"

JABOLINSKY
>What did he say?

HUSSERL
>What did he say? He said I had broken off
>The blossoming bough of philosophers. He said because of me
>Nietzsche, Hegel, and Kant would not have a home.
>He blamed me directly for philosophy's fall
>Behind psychoanalysis and sociology and anthropology as a study
>>that would interest a sane person.
>He said concepts of form, substance, and essence would pay a
>>heavy price
>For my rackety defoliation of their perfect branches. He blamed
>>me for everything and
>I went home and threw out Croce, Whitehead, and Kant,
>Because I think he is right,
>And now I am going to throw myself into the sea—

JABOLINSKY
>Don't! Wait—

HUSSERL

> —Of thought, to see if we can't come up with something better
>> than that
> Poor out-of-date, rickety, clanky philosophy!

JABOLINSKY

> Oh you are a man after my heart
> And I wish you success!

HUSSERL

> I pray that that success will come as Substance,
> And not merely as Form.
> Evelyn may be lonely sometimes . . .
> But now I am embarked!

JABOLINSKY

> Good luck, Husserl!

HUSSERL

> Dear friend, farewell.

(He leaves.)

Angels

(People slowly come on and go off stage, one by one, carrying big white banners. They are like people carrying signs in a parade or on a picket line or at a political demonstration. There is something noble and beautiful about it, suggestive of a heavenly intervention, as of angels. On the banners, as they appear, one can read the following messages:)

DID ANCIENT GREEKS HAVE DIGESTIVE SYSTEMS?

DO BUTTERFLIES SOMETIMES ACCIDENTALLY CANCEL STAMPS?

IS YOUR CONSTITUTION STRONG ENOUGH TO WITHSTAND THE PROBLEMS OF THE PRESENT DAY?

IF MARY KINGSLEY, AFTER WRITING *Travels in West Africa*, HAD NOT GONE TO AFRICA A SECOND TIME, WOULD SHE STILL BE ALIVE TODAY? WOULD SHE HAVE WRITTEN ANOTHER BOOK AS GOOD AS THE FIRST ONE?

IS RUDOLF NUREYEV TO GEORGE BALANCHINE AS A DROMEDARY IS TO A CAMEL?

SHOULD THERE BE ATOMIC FUEL?

IS LYRIC POETRY AN ADVANCE, A RETRACTION, OR AN ESCAPE? OR NONE OF THESE?

IS IT MAINLY FRAGMENTS, OR ENTITIES, THAT MAKE UP THE COLOSSUS OF OUR LIVES?

WHO, IF ANYONE, WOULD YOU LIKE TO BE CLOSE TO YOU FOR AN UNLIMITED PERIOD OF TIME?

HOW MANY COATS ARE ON THE GABONESE RACK?

WHAT COULD BEST DISTRACT YOU FROM THE REAL, SAD, MANIPULATED LIFE OF GOATS?

WERE YOU HAPPIER A WEEK (MONTH, YEAR) AGO? AND HOW CAN YOU TELL?

DID A FIG FALL ON AN UNMENTIONED STONE?

CLOWNS LOOK SAD TO MAKE US LAUGH. WHO LOOKS HAPPY TO MAKE US CRY? ANGELS?

FOR ONE FIVE-MINUTE SPAN IN MEXICO CITY DID YOU FEEL THAT EVERYTHING WAS POSSIBLE? DID YOU RECORD THIS FEELING? FROM WHERE, DO YOU THINK, DID IT COME?

DOES SILENCE MOVE YOU? OR IS IT TRUER TO SAY THAT THE WATER IS MOVED BY THE BOAT?

IS YOUR HOPE INDEPENDENT OF YOUR SENSE OF CONTINGENT REALITY?

CAN YOU GIVE ME FIVE CENTS?

IF MARY MAGDALENE IS THE SOUL AND RED RIDING HOOD THE HEART, IS BOZO THE BRAIN OF THESE SCENES? OR CAN IT BE MAO TSE-TUNG AS A CORPSE?

LITERARY INFLUENCE—ARE YOU DISTURBED BY IT? WHAT ABOUT OTHER KINDS OF INFLUENCE?

WHY DO HENS HAVE EGGS AND NOT BABIES?

WHO ARE THE TRUE MEN AND WHO ARE THE TRUE WOMEN, AND WHICH DO YOU PREFER?

WHAT DID RAMAKRISHNA GIVE TO VITKA FOR KALIDASSA'S BIRTHDAY?

IF YOU WERE TO DIE THIS EVENING, WHAT WOULD BE THE THING YOU LIKED MOST ABOUT LIFE SO FAR?

(Now a crew of police, or plainclothes RULE ENFORCERS *of some kind, come on and chase the* BANNER-BEARERS *away.)*

RULE ENFORCERS
> Here, here, get out of here, all of you, you know it's not permitted! Go on now, get away!

(One last BANNER-BEARER, AN ANGEL, *comes out with one last banner:)*

DO YOU BELIEVE IN SIGNS? ARE YOU AFFECTED BY THEM AT ALL?

The Underground Army

(Completely dark, under the earth. Hundreds, even thousands, of CLAY SOL-
DIERS *appear very dimly—among them,* HO *and* HA.*)*

HO

> They say Chen Ko is coming to organize us, the Underground
>   Army,
> To fight.

HA

> Against whom? And how can we fight? We are clay, we are earth.

HO

> To fight against the Han Emperor, who,
> Jealous of the power of the underground troops of his Imperial
>   predecessor, wishes to destroy us.
> He will come down to chop us
> And to chip us into subservience to his will.

HA

> In that case we must fight. But HOW
> Shall we fight? Since we are not living beings.

HO

> That depends,
> Perhaps, on how we are thought of.
> If someone, if only one person, believes that we exist,
> That we live, and that we matter, then, perhaps,
> For him or for her, we WILL exist and will be able to fight.

(Enter CHEN KO.*)*

CHEN KO

> Hail and hello on this hot, dusty day, my marvelous clay soldiers.
> Time has come that we shall have to battle for our lives,
> For ourselves and for the glory of our Emperor
> Which is still undimmed.

HA

I do, sometimes, still feel the Emperor among us—
Though not always. But, tell us,
How can we fight?

HO

Listen—

(Aboveground a GIRL'S VOICE *is heard.)*

GIRL'S VOICE

I believe in the underground soldiers. They will fight to protect us.
I know they will. They are brave. They will fight for China!

(A tremendous din.)

CHEN KO

Here come the armies of Jaing Chai, Emperor de Han.

(Enter a raging HORDE *headed by* HAN EMPEROR.*)*

HAN EMPEROR

Come, break those bodies, break them into dust!
No one shall rule in the Underworld but Jaing Chai Han!!

(In the darkness, a noisy, confusing, violent battle. Finally, it ends.)

GIRL'S VOICE

Oh, my clay soldiers—may they, so brave, remain!

The Mediterranean

MEDITERRANEAN
    I am the Mediterranean, I wash on all my shores.
    I am gull of the Adriatic, Vinland away from the Azores
    With light-blue waves my windows, rocks my doors.
    I am the Mediterranean.
    On merely hearing my name
    People become excited and kick all the same
    Jumping all around thinking "Mediterranean!"
    Oh I am she
    Perhaps it is in Venice that I'm most permeated
    And most permeate
    There my eyelashes go up to the tops of buildings
    There my smiles lead merchantmen to the sea (further out)
    There I am the first basket of transportation
    I am the Mediterranean
    I am that calming sea
    That kills (with my marshlands).

(Enter ITALY *and* SPAIN, *galantuomini, who bow to her.)*

    And my peninsulas gather for me
    Gold and fantastical stores
    From the ends of this planet and develop for me
    Strong and individual personalities

*(*SPAIN *shows himself to be a matador,* ITALY *an operatic tenor.)*

    So that I can go to sleep in them
    And wake up knowing I am still the Sea
    That precludes uninclusive history
    And greets the most amazing of forms.

(Enter the TIDES.*)*

>   Say, Tides, am I not in each Italian man's, in each Spanish
>   woman's heart?

TIDES
>   Yes, Regina, you are.

MEDITERRANEAN
>   I wash
>   On all these shores!

Now the blue expanse of water begins to fill up with what is found in modern harbors: cranes, derricks, oil tankers, tugboats, and so on. The boats hoot, the water becomes a little dirty. The MEDITERRANEAN *looks at all this with concern, and, withdrawing to one side, expresses her fears.)*

MEDITERRANEAN
>   But what are these, but what is this I see
>   Moving upon and settling down in me? Oh cause of fear!
>   Derricks, and tankers, floating petrol bankers,
>   Riggers and clankers—what they may do to me
>   I feel some cause to fear. Shall my great Mediterranean
>   Balm be swept aside? and death go with my tide?
>   O gods of earth and light and of the sea
>   And of the air, of which I am the bride, tell me:
>   Can the great sea of my great self abide?

(Enter TOMMY TIME. *All is silent.)*

TOMMY TIME
>   Let Tommy Time decide!

(He leaps into the water.)

Gospel Red Riding Noh Tanayachi

(On the left is LITTLE RED RIDING HOOD*'s house, with a woodland path out-side its door. On the right is a* CHORUS OF DEER. *All the characters sing their lines gospel-style; the singing of the* CHORUS *is sometimes soft, sometimes jubilant.)*

MOTHER
Oh Little Red Raheedin
    Hoood
Oh Little Red Raheedin
    Hoood

CHORUS
Yes, she
Yes, she
Yes, she
Gwine be comin'
    along

LITTLE RED RIDING HOOD
Yas yas ah comin' along
Goin' to gran mamma's
    house yes yes yes yes
    yes yes
Yeah, granmuthah's house!

Oh Lord! Yes, she
Yes, she
Yes, she
Gwine be comin'
    along

MOTHER
Oh Lil Red Raheedin Hoood
Yas yas yes yes yes

*(*LITTLE RED RIDING HOOD *walks along the woodland path. Halfway she meets the* WOLF.*)*

LITTLE RED RIDING HOOD
Comin' along
Doan fine dat wuff
Gran granmuthah's place
Oh yeah! oh yeah!

CHORUS
Comin' along
Yes, she
Yes, she
Is comin'
    along!

WOLF
    Lil Red Raheedin Hood,
      whachu

Whachu, whachu
Whachu gopp in de baskeck

LITTLE RED RIDING HOOD
    Oh yes
    I go fine de restin place
    Wif my
    Granmuthah

CHORUS
Yas, wachu
Wolf know? Who
Who are you?

(The scene changes to GRANDMOTHER'*s house. The* WOLF *is in bed in* GRAND-
MOTHER'*s clothes.* LITTLE RED RIDING HOOD *enters.)*

WOLF
I no grandma but de wuff
    an I gwine eat you
Yes yeah yes

CHORUS
Know who
No, she doan know who
Hoo hoo hoo
She doan know who

(Enter WOODSMAN.*)*

Oh but oh but who dat

Yes, yes

WOODSMAN
I's de WOODSMAN
Ho ho, yeah!

Yes, yes
Lil Red Ridin' Hood

LITTLE RED RIDING HOOD
    Where's my granmuthah?
    No, yes!

GRANDMOTHER
    Wolf eat me—woo woo woo
    Ooh ooh ooh ooh

*(At this moment, the play abruptly changes in style, becoming a traditional
Japanese Noh drama. The* SHITE, *the principal character in a Noh play, is*
LITTLE RED RIDING HOOD; *the* WAKI, *the secondary character, is the* WOODS-
MAN. LITTLE RED RIDING HOOD *comes center stage to recite the following
speech. In doing so, she is able, in classic Noh fashion, to relive a tormenting
episode of her past and, in the end, to find absolution and peace.)*

SHITE (LITTLE RED RIDING HOOD)
    She set out from home, ah! cursed, burdened
    With basket, meeting,
    She—beautiful young girl—a wolf
    Then coupled and crashing, led this
    Monster to house of honored and ancient
    Grandmother Kai Se Nan, this is her house.
    "You must choose between me
    And your grandmother." Your teeth
    Flash. Ah ah! The knees buckle, the head,
    Faint, the young body falls to the floor
    Doomed by lust.

(At this point the CHORUS *takes over the* SHITE's *speech; it is clear that it is still* LITTLE RED RIDING HOOD's *words that are being heard. The events being described are acted out in dumb show by the characters, in the formal style of Noh drama.)*

CHORUS
    A woodsman comes, seeing
    The shame, wolf on maiden, extracting
    A knife kills
    But not her who should
    Be killed, she guilty, but
    The wolf, not wholly
    Innocent he but pushed by his nature only. She
    Indecisive, murderess, lies there. He,
    Woodsman, sympathizing, desiring, then
    Takes her in one last
    Act of lust, she obeying, wolf
    Rises from near-death to scratch bite kill
    Woodsman, he too now dead, all
    They dead she
    To her knees
    Rises, seeing, horrified
    This bloody sight.

(Now LITTLE RED RIDING HOOD *takes over her speech again. The dumb show stops.)*

48

SHITE (LITTLE RED RIDING HOOD)
    I am
    The cause! Now,
    On my knees, I make
    Amends—good-bye. With this
    Knife, parting, freedom,
    Absolution.

(LITTLE RED RIDING HOOD *stabs herself.*)

WAKI (WOODSMAN)
    It is at
    An end. Her
    Suffering has ceased.
    Now the October wind
    Blows coolly through the dwelling of Tokani Tokanise.

Robert Wilson Riding Hood

(RED RIDING HOOD *moves with agonizing slowness across the stage. The* WOLF *stands stage right explaining something to an invisible companion.)*

WOLF

So I said that it was her perfect right to take a package, which is what I understood she was carrying, to the home of an old relative, but that I, too, had the right to have some fun. After all, a person has the right to have a little fun. I said that it was her perfect right to take . . .

(This speech may be repeated as long as the director likes.)

(When RED RIDING HOOD *almost reaches the vicinity of the* WOLF *she begins moving backward at the same pace at which she was moving forward. There is music of trains, loud factory whistles, and escaping steam.)*

In China None

(COOK walks onstage, as if just coming out of a theatre in which she has seen the two previous plays.)

COOK
> In China we have none of this stuff
> Because it seems like crazy.
> A recognition of the historical impulse
> In a simple Marxist way makes aestheticians lazy.
> So—it will come or it will not come. In any case, it makes no
> difference now.

The Black Spanish Costume

(A Royal Ball in Spain in the sixteenth century.)

MAIN BLACK SPANISH COSTUME *(female)*
    I am the black costume, the costume of Spain—
    I dominate Europe. You cannot gain
    Admission to a royal celebration
    Unless you wear me. It's useless to complain.
    Oh, victory is mine! I am the costume
    The black costume of Spain.
    And I will last forever. Eternal is my reign.

OTHER BLACK COSTUMES
    Eternal be your reign!

(Enter the PINK FRENCH DRESS.*)*

BLACK COSTUME *(male)*
    And who are you?

PINK FRENCH DRESS
    A pink French dress.

BLACK COSTUME
    How beautiful you are.
    Would you honor me with a dance?

PINK FRENCH DRESS
    I'd love to dance.

(The male BLACK COSTUME *and the* PINK FRENCH DRESS *dance.)*

BLACK COSTUME
    It is because of you
    That we shall be undone.

OTHER BLACK COSTUMES *(softly, together)*
    Oh, we feel a catastrophic change.

BLACK COSTUME
How did you get here?

PINK FRENCH DRESS
Why, we all come from France.
Upon the backs of dolls we came from France.
I *like* to dance. Look, here we are.

(Enter many PINK FRENCH DRESSES. *Each goes and stands in front of a* BLACK SPANISH COSTUME, *as if preparing to dance. When the* PINK FRENCH DRESSES *next move, however, the* BLACK SPANISH COSTUMES *have disappeared.)*

Similar Events

(Enter the FIRST CHARACTERS: "BAD" MARY MAGDALENE, *an* OLD-FASHIONED STEAM ENGINE, *a* HORSE, MILLET, *a* SAINT PAINTED BY GIOTTO *(possibly St. Francis), a* HUGE HAND, *the* CARPATHIAN MOUNTAINS, HOMER, MONGOLIAN FLATLANDS, *and others. They stand around chatting with each other as at a party.)*

FIRST CHARACTERS
Chanda chak, chak chak, chanda chak chak chak,
Chanda chanda, chak chanda chak chak, chak chanda, etc.

VOICES OF THE SECOND CHARACTERS *(offstage)*
We're coming, at different times, we're on our way.

FIRST CHARACTERS
Chanda chak chak chak, nothing will ever change,
Tout restera le même, niente cambiera chandy chak
Chandy chak chak

(The SECOND CHARACTERS *appear at the side of the stage. They are the* GOOD MARY MAGDALENE, *a* MODERN STEAM ENGINE, *an* AUTOMOBILE, *an* EAR OF CORN, *a* SAINT PAINTED BY PIERO DELLA FRANCESCA, *a* BIG KNIFE AND FORK, *the* CARPATHIAN MOUNTAINS, TENNYSON, BEIJING, *and others. All at once, they come out and one by one stand in front of their corresponding* FIRST CHARACTERS. *When the* SECOND CHARACTER *then moves, the* FIRST CHARACTER *is seen to have disappeared as the* BLACK SPANISH COSTUMES *disappeared in the previous play. The* SECOND CHARACTERS *make different sounds, actually two different kinds—half of them say [1] and half [2].)*

(1)
Sim sam sam cheroo chim sim charam soum cham chim
Eeyouchim cham

(2)
Goggor aggog foggag goorg gogganeggaboggagaged

(A slight rumble is heard offstage, and some THIRD CHARACTERS *start becoming visible in the wings as the play ends. The* THIRD CHARACTERS *include the*

MARY MAGDALENE OF THESE PLAYS—*neither "good" nor "bad" but just "coming along"*—*a* COMPUTER, *an* AIRPLANE, FROZEN ORANGE JUICE, GUERNICA, *a* CUISINART, *the* CARPATHIAN MOUNTAINS, T. S. ELIOT, *and* MAO TSE-TUNG.)

Gospel Toothbrush

(PAUL CÉZANNE is painting a still life. Perhaps to help his concentration, he sings softly, as he works, in a gospel style. His singing may at times be backed up by a CHORUS OF OTHER PAINTERS and/or BIG PAINTBRUSHES.)

CÉZANNE

    Yeh yeh yeh yeh yes yas yeah
    How ole in de mawning you gwine use it
      Hey hey ho hah
    Gospel toothbrush!
      Yeah!
    So many brissle wan you fine
      Ho yeah yes yes yes yas oh now
    Hole him up straight yeah an ben head down
      Yeah!
    Gospel toothbrush, take your time
    Brush, yes mm hmm
    Brosse aux dents, oh yes
    Oh yes, yes, fine,
    Brosse aux—mm hmm
    So fine hey hey . . . hey hey . . . hey . . .
    Brush of mine, Lord yes,
    Now done
    All done
    For today, yes yes, hmm mmm—

(His work for the day finished, he puts down his brushes and leaves.)

Permanently

(There is an atmosphere of grammar and elementary school. The scene is a city sidewalk and street. In the first part of the play the doings of the ADJECTIVE *and the* NOUNS *are acted out on one part of the stage while, on another, the* PARENTS *and* CHILDREN *watch and make comments.)*

MAN
> The Nouns are clustered in the street

WOMAN
> An Adjective walks past

CHILD
> Oh, she kisses the Nouns!

MAN
> The principal will be in a rage

WOMAN
> Look here he comes he is indeed a tower

(The PRINCIPAL *totters in.)*

PRINCIPAL
> Adjective, Nouns, get back in the textbook
> Otherwise we won't include you in the next book—

WOMAN
> But the Nouns are struck, moved, changed.

MAN
> I think they've fallen in love with the Adjective
> In any event they say, "You can't write a book of any kind without
> us
> At least of any size. So go away. Give us our liberty today.
> We've seen an Adjective and all for us is changed."

(The PRINCIPAL *hobbles off.)*

CHILD

Oh look

The principal is hobbling away. Defeat is in his look. Maybe he
will be cheered up by Cook.

(Darkness, dawn, morning light. It's the next day. VERB *drives up in his car.)*

VERB

I am a Verb. My car is at the curb. And I'm driving away.
Adjective and Nouns, jump in!

*(*ADJECTIVE *and* NOUNS *get in the car.* OTHER PARTS OF SPEECH *run onstage.)*

OTHER PARTS OF SPEECH

Oh, take us, too!

(They get in. The car drives off slowly.)

MAN

They've created the Sentence! Come, let's read what it says.

(Behind the VERB*'s car flutters a big paper pennant with these words on it: "You have enchanted me with a single kiss/Which can never be undone/Until the destruction of language.")*

The Burning Mystery of Anna

(It is 1951. The scene is a modest dansing *in Aix-en-Provence.)*

JEAN

>Do you see that girl over there?
>She's Corsican.

ANNA

>Love is my name.

KENNETH

>What shall I say?

JEAN

>Ask her to dance?

KENNETH

>My head, my arms, my shoulders feeling strange.

JEAN

>See that girl over there. Anna.
>Ask her to dance.

KENNETH

>Islands of awkward animals.

JEAN

>Witticisms strewn about—and vanished.
>Improve with age. Dance.

KENNETH

>Never be the same.

ANNA

>My name is Anna.
>I don't know how to kiss.

KENNETH

>Why am I at this age—twenty-six?

ANNA

>I, I'm nineteen—to remember?

ANNA
Good fortune, dance.

JEAN
Else die, the same.

Départ Malgache

AFRICA
>Madagascar, why are you leaving?

MADAGASCAR
>I don't know.
>But I do know this is two hundred fifty MILLION years ago,
>And I have to go.

AFRICA
>Lemur-filled and enormous island, where will you go?

MADAGASCAR
>I don't know—I think just out there in the sea—
>To save my lemurs I have to go . . .

AFRICA
>Good-bye!

(MADAGASCAR *floats out into the Indian Ocean.*)

>O addio, dolce Madagascar!

(*Malagasy music.*)

On the Edge

(A street and a town square in which anything is possible.)

STENDHAL
    I'm looking for Dan.

*(*DAN*, riding on a goat, enters. He gets off the goat.)*

DAN
    Here I am.

STENDHAL
    It is time I got to know myself.

(Botticelli's VENUS *appears.)*

VENUS
    I am Venus, rising from the Sea!
    Where does each moment's deepest meaning lie?

STENDHAL
    It's in the goat—

*(*GOAT *trots forward.)*

DAN
    And in the footnote.

(Traces a message on the sidewalk with one foot.)

    It lamps what is not to come

(With his foot he now erases the message.)

    As well as what is—
    A bannister of bones

*(*SKELETON *appears.)*

And a hat.

(A hat is thrown onstage.)

It felt like forever—

(Enter CHRISTINE *and* EDWARD*.)*

EDWARD
It feels "interrogating flat."

CHRISTINE
It feels shown.

STENDHAL
Vanning about and straggling.

EDWARD
Why is it so unknown?

(A car drives up. One at a time, each character gets in the car, then gets out of it and walks off, saying:)

ALL
Getting out of the car and going back.

Smoking Hamlet

HAMLET
> To be, or not to be: that is the question.
> Whether 'tis nobler in the mind to suffer
> The slings and arrows of outrageous fortune
> Or to take arms against a sea of troubles
> And by opposing end them.

(HAMLET *lights a cigarette, inhales, exhales, and walks offstage.*)

La Comtesse de Bercy Hamlet

(Enter, en toute élégance, Anne, COMTESSE DE BERCY.*)*

COMTESSE
    To be, or not to be: that is the question.
    Whether 'tis nobler in the mind to suffer
    The slings and arrows of outrageous fortune
    Or to take arms against a sea of troubles
    And by opposing end them.

(At the end, a strong wind blows and her clothes swirl all about her.)

Team Hamlet

(Six TEAM MEMBERS *stand in a line facing the audience. Each says, in order, one syllable of Hamlet's "To be, or not to be" speech. After every six syllables, or after every poetic line, the* TEAM MEMBERS *change their posture—they sit, kneel, turn sideways, stand backward, lie down, etc.)*

Little Red Riding Hamlet

(LITTLE RED RIDING HOOD*'s house; outside it, a forest; then* GRAND-MOTHER*'s house. While an offstage* VOICE *recites Hamlet's speech, the story of Little Red Riding Hood is acted out in dumb show.)*

VOICE
> To be, or not to be: that is the question.

(LITTLE RED RIDING HOOD*'s* MOTHER *gives her a basket.* LITTLE RED RID-ING HOOD *leaves home.)*

VOICE
> Whether 'tis nobler in the mind to suffer

(LITTLE RED RIDING HOOD *encounters the* WOLF.*)*

VOICE
> The slings and arrows of outrageous fortune

(LITTLE RED RIDING HOOD *walks on to* GRANDMOTHER*'s house, goes in and finds the* WOLF *in bed disguised as* GRANDMOTHER, *and questions him.)*

VOICE
> Or to take arms against a sea of troubles

(The WOLF *attacks* LITTLE RED RIDING HOOD. *She cries out. The* WOODS-MAN *arrives.)*

VOICE
> And by opposing end them.

(The WOODSMAN *kills the* WOLF, *splits him open, rescues* GRANDMOTHER, *and all is well.)*

Hamlet Rebus

(A very big, white EGG *is onstage.)*

HAMLET
> To be, or not to be: that is the question.

*(*CHICKEN *comes out of* EGG. HAMLET *smiles, and continues.)*

> Whether 'tis nobler in the mind to suffer

(Enraged FORTUNE *figure comes on and attacks* HAMLET *and the* CHICKEN *with slung stones and arrows.)*

> The slings and arrows of outrageous fortune

(After slinging and shooting at HAMLET, FORTUNE *disappears.)*

> Or to take arms against a sea of troubles

(Big noise of waves, tempest, crashing, screams and moans. HAMLET *draws his sword.)*

> And by opposing end them.

(He rushes off. The sounds cease.)

Transposed Hamlet

(HAMLET, *wearing avant-garde clothes.*)

HAMLET
>Tube heat, or nog tube heat: data's congestion.
>Ladder tricks snow blur Hindu mine dew sulphur
>Tea slinks end harrows have ow! Cages portion
>Orc tube rake harms hay canst a Z oeuf bubbles
>Ant ply cop posy kingdom.

(He goes crazy.)

Aux Seins de Mandarine

(A public square in Port-au-Prince, Haiti.)

FIELLA
>In Haiti when I was a fresh young girl
>How I used to dance and my head was in a whirl
>Over such dancing.
>One day they'd find me and carry me away
>In Haiti, in Haiti, oppressive dictatorship holiday.
>>Tonton Macoute
>>Is listening to you!
>>Tonton Macoute
>>Is listening to you!
>The roads have improved—
>There used to be no roads!
>>Salads and fish!
>Marabout de mon coeur—

MARCHING MEN
>In Haiti at this time
>In Haiti at this time
>We come from government!
>We come from government at this time!
>We are marching at this time—
>From bad government
>We come from government at this time!

*(*MARCHING MEN *do a rending sort of dance, then leave. The scene changes to Senegal—Dakar—where the* HAITIAN EXILES *speak.)*

HAITIAN EXILES
>In exile, we restrict our moods.
>In exile, we have certain aptitudes.
>In exile, the hot thrashing of the day
>Is as irritating as elsewhere
>Though politically it is as a holiday.
>If we could rush at them and kill them

And then go back,
We would still not be back
Not be really, really back
After these years of exile.

Different Rooms Doctor

(This takes place in many different rooms of the same building. The only speaking character is the DOCTOR, *who goes from room to room, making one short speech in each, to his patients. The* AUDIENCE *follows the* DOCTOR *from room to room.)*

DOCTOR
You have a heart attack. (*Musingly*) If it's the bullfighter.

*(*DOCTOR *goes on to the next room—and to another room for each of these succeeding speeches.)*

How young are you? Hmmmm. Just about Red-Riding-Hood size. Summer—yes, it was summer when we spoke. I remember. We were near Tawai Nakimo.

Cast-iron cover. Elfred the Dancer? I can't explain this. There isn't enough air in the room. . . .

Egypt to see me? I don't know. Edward and Christine? What's "Tommy Time"?

Come back next year. Oh, yes, sure, I'll think it over. But the clay soldiers—perhaps it's just as well.

Known elements of a car: engine, steering wheel, crankshaft, and drive. Happiness was here? When? While we were alive?

I don't think I want (thank you) a cocktail. But you look startling in your black Spanish dress.

Thank you for the star. I never really knew about shining before I got it.

What, what, what's that? Oh, you have a high fever. Quetzalcoatl, master of the storm.

Get into some of this and out of that other. Emolument? That's rather one of Hamlet's type of words.

The mule doctor is on vacation. I'm here to chime for Cook.

(The DOCTOR *goes into the hall.)*

Science, good-bye! And, also, to economic fiction!

(He opens the door and goes outside.)

I am—I was—the Doctor. But Doctor am no more! Look at the
    sky—
Oh, medicine of that blue, straight nose!

The Chinese Rivers

YELLOW
> I am the Yellow River

YANGTSE
> I am the Yangtse, great to view

YELLOW and YANGTSE *(together, or alternating)*
> Here above Shanghai we meet
> No far from Han Kow
> No far from Soo Chow
> No far from the feet
> Of the white, bouldery mountains
> No far from the seat
> Of China's grain—
> Oh, industry
> Of ants, swiftness
> Of animals, and initiative of humans!
> Let our resources be used to produce
> Power for the influence to very good life in our country
> That has always been the center of the world!

Christine, Edward, and the Cube

(A street in Mexico City. EDWARD *and* CHRISTINE, *walking together, encounter the* AVANT-GARDE CUBE.*)*

CUBE
> Hello there!

CHRISTINE
> I'm confused.
> Where used to be a building
> Now there's an isolated, shining door.

CUBE
> You two—

EDWARD
> Yes. And where there were flowers
> Look, steel spikes. But
> Your hand is still as soft
> In mine as it was before.

CHRISTINE
> But I have a kind of wart on it.
> Do you really like my hands?

EDWARD
> Look, Christine. That explains it. It's the Avant-Garde.

CUBE
> In downtown Mexico City's commanding uproar
> I have a temple of art, but it may vanish in a second,
> Depending on the government and on taste.

EDWARD
> She's right. And it may depend on our government, too.
> God knows what it's about to do in this part of the world! . . .
> Though I am melting to you. And with you.

CHRISTINE

> I to you, too. Maybe we can find a cross-
> Way between the political and our life
> And maybe we cannot. Oh
> Edward, who knows? The main
> Problem now seems to be how old
> You are and young I am. My
> Step-parents are going to flip—

CUBE

> And I am the Avant-Garde.
> Follow me, and you'll end up on a still tip
> Of a frozen wing
> In the acrid penumbra
> Of magnesiated space. Come on!

(She leads them off.)

From the M'Vett

SCENE I. *Army Headquarters tent.* CAPTAIN FOGG *at the desk,* STAFF SERGEANT MILCH *standing.*

FOGG

Have you been able to find out what's wrong with the code
On these fucking rockets? They trail always into some African place
And go boom. They are not hitting their fucking god-damned targets.

MILCH

I know the problem but I'm damned if I can see the solution.

FOGG

Get Sergeant Dawb in here.

MILCH

Yes sir.

*(*MILCH *exits, re-enters with* DAWB.*)*

FOGG

Dawb?

DAWB

Sir?

FOGG

Do you know what's happening to these motherfucking rockets?

DAWB

Dey am heat seekin, am deys nock?

FOGG *(mocking his accent)*

Yacks, dam is. But what the fuck has that got to do with it?

DAWB

Everything, My Lord, if you believe me. Nothing, if you do not.
(He pauses, as if searching for something in his thoughts.) I think there
is some place in Africa that is attracting them—

An old story I heard once, part of the M'Vett,
Our Gabonese epic poem, something about a stove. . . .

FOGG
> Dawb, do you think you could find that stove?

DAWB *(saluting)*
> Yessir . . . (*He starts to leave, then stops; to himself*) I go, but with a
> divided heart. My great-grandfather was Behanzu . . . the
> Shark.

(Toot toot of Congo boats and jungle wind through the trees.)

SCENE 2. *In a heavy mist.*

MAN
> How did it end with Dawb and the Stove of Peace?

SECOND MAN
> I don't know. They never found out.

(The TWO MEN *leave. The mist clears, revealing* DAWB *and* M'BAMU.*)*

DAWB
> I am sitting beside it.

M'BAMU
> Dawb is sitting beside it here with me.
> He married one of my daughters and he sits beside it,
> He is sitting beside the Stove of Peace.
> Later you will see it.

The Arrival of Homosexuality in Greece, or The Fagabond

*(A Greek island. Two men—*MINETOS *and* ARCHILOKOS—*are standing on the shore.* ARISTIPPUS *arrives from the sea.)*

ARISTIPPUS (THE FAGABOND)
What's the name of this island?

MINETOS
Hydra.

ARISTIPPUS
Where is it?

MINETOS
In the Aegean, in Greece.

ARISTIPPUS
I love it, I love that, I love you.

*(*ARISTIPPUS *embraces* MINETOS.*)*

MINETOS
What? Are you mad? I'm a MAN. I love WOMEN. Women love ME. Not men men. Get away from me. Archilokos, take him! We must bind him and bring him to trial. Frankly, I feel like having him killed.

ARISTIPPUS
Just for a little hug? Don't be such a bear! You like it, admit it. I know you do.

MINETOS
Actually I don't. Get away. Archilokos—

*(*ARCHILOKOS *lunges forward as if pushed,* MINETOS *also.)*

ARCHILOKOS
Wait. Something's happening.

MINETOS
Somebody, something, gave me a shove.

ARCHILOKOS
Me too.

ARISTIPPUS
Well, sillies, what do you think? There's more to me, you know, than
MEETS THE GUY. Ho ha ha ha!

MINETOS
But what, who is it?

(Suddenly, in their midst, beside ARISTIPPUS, *the god* EROS *is revealed. It was
he who pushed the two men.)*

EROS
Beware! Beware! Be airy! For I am LOVE.
Know that this is a real thing. Have respect for it.
Life has need of it. Love must be free.

MINETOS
Eros! But it goes against the grain—

EROS
The grain isn't everything, Minetos. Remember that.

*(*EROS *vanishes in a red-pink golden fire.)*

ARISTIPPUS
(*putting on a white beard*) You can call me Psyche, if you want. Oh
no! (*tugging at the beard*) That's entirely the wrong thing for her!
(*laughs*)

MINETOS *and* ARCHILOKOS
(*smiling*) Oh well, all right.

Watteau's Reputation

(The Sorbonne.)

RAMON FERNANDEZ
>It's Watteau's problem that he was
>Ahead of his time and so appreciated only later
>And then in the work of epigones with less talent
>In a more watered-down form of his work. Then only really
>Valued correctly in the nineteenth century, when
>The themes of his paintings were hopelessly out-of-date.

MARY MAGDALENE
>We should go back in time and tell him
>Of his high stature now.

CUPIDON
>Yes. I
>Will go with you, Mary Magdalene.

RAMON FERNANDEZ
>Good luck—and bring me news.

(The scene shifts to WATTEAU'*s atelier.* WATTEAU *is painting a group of* LADIES *and* GENTLEMEN.*)*

WATTEAU
>Finally it's finished—another Fête Galante!

(Enter the PLAGUE.*)*

PLAGUE
>I am the Bubonic Plague.

WATTEAU
>Get away from me!

*(*LADIES *and* GENTLEMEN *push* PLAGUE *offstage and follow after it. Enter* MARY MAGDALENE *and* CUPIDON.*)*

WATTEAU

    Ah! Mary Magdalene and Cupidon. I've been waiting
For you, sit down. Have some coffee. I'm going to make of you
The greatest painting I have ever made: Le départ pour le
Cythère—or . . . du Cythère? That is,
Are the people going to Cytherea paradise or leaving it?

MARY MAGDALENE

    Yes, which?

WATTEAU

    I don't know. Going to it, I think—

(He paints.)

    No—leaving it.
Actually, no—going to it—No! Leav—

CUPIDON

    We came here to tell you something else—

(Re-enter the PLAGUE, *leading the* LADIES *and* GENTLEMEN; *crossing the stage, it sweeps away* WATTEAU, MARY MAGDALENE, *and* CUPIDON *in its wake.)*

Hippopotamus Migration in Africa

(The HIPPOS *speak, as they move, migratorily, across a semidarkened stage.)*

We the Hippopotamuses
Are hurtling down
Through Africa
Toward the Sea.
We shall never reach the Sea.
The Sea's not meant for us. Our destiny
Takes us toward protracted stays in jungle
Where to stay
We have to stay in streams
In inland river streams
All day, and only at night
Pull up our lonely, lovely heads
To climb to land—and grass—
To eat—
Then back
To slimy scummy water above our back
At dawn
When the hard day begins,
When the hard hippo-
Potamus-head-destroying
Day begins.

(Very bright sunlight.)

Wittgenstein, or Bravo, Dr. Wittgenstein!

WITTGENSTEIN
    The only things that we can say
    Are the things that are already said
    By existing actions—
    For example: I am walking today.
    It cannot be said
    This walk is taking me forward
    Or, I am the subject, or the form, of this walk.
    Then, proscriptively,
    The only things that we *should* say
    Are those that we can say. I am taking a walk.
    What cannot be said with clarity
    Should not—and cannot—be said—
    Thus I must conclude
    That the unsayable
    Has no further chance of being said—
    And, this being so,

    Our old philosopher's dream is unattainable
    And can never come true.

Tadeusz Kantor and the Duck

Enter a large DUCK *dressed in black.* TADEUSZ KANTOR, *the noted Polish director, is to one side of the stage, directing in a furtive sort of way. The* DUCK *starts to die. Then, suddenly, the* DUCK *sees* KANTOR *and begins "directing"* KANTOR. KANTOR *staggers around the stage, then dies in the center of the stage. The* DUCK *sits on him and quacks. Then, to loud, funereal music,* KANTOR *is reborn. He and the* DUCK *go to opposite ends of the stage, then run into each other with a crash. Both fall dead. Then each gets up and, with an ordinary walk, leaves the stage. Two or four* GHOULS *or* SKELETONS *come out holding up a placard that says,* "TADEUSZ KANTOR AND THE DUCK." *Loud, funereal music, and the play begins again.*

The Theatre at Epidauros

(It is very dry and very hot. On the stage of the ancient Greek theatre, Greek ACTORS *are rehearsing lines from tragedies.)*

FIRST ACTOR
> The tender body of your first-born son
> Is what you have eaten here—

SECOND ACTOR
> As he died, I was splattered
> By the dark red fountain of his blood,
> And I was happy, as if I were a garden
> Nourished by the fresh spring rain.

THIRD ACTOR
> My brother is dead. Let's stomp on his corpse!

(A LITTLE DOG *runs onstage and nips at the* ACTORS' *heels.)*

LITTLE DOG
> Argh argh argh argh greeouw!

FOURTH ACTOR
> Oh, push me with one unconvulsive leap
> Against the point of this death-dealing blade!

LITTLE DOG
> Reeouw rrgh!

FOURTH ACTOR
> Get that dog

THIRD ACTOR
> Out of here

FIRST AND SECOND ACTORS
> Get that noisome dog
> Out of the Theatre of Epidauros!

(The god of medicine, AESCULAPIUS, *comes onstage and picks up the* LITTLE DOG *in his arms.)*

AESCULAPIUS
Come, my child, I shall shelter and guard you.
No longer will anyone forget to take you out.
And we will take long pleasant walks together—
We'll leave this sickening theatre alone
Where there is talk of nothing but family murder
And devastation, relatives eating each other—
It is enough to make even me, Aesculapius, sick at heart. . . . You,
dog,
Are the healthiest, most natural thing
I have seen in this Epidauros Theatre in a long, long time.

(The memory of his wife, who died young, momentarily comes back to AESCU-LAPIUS.*)*

Oh, Xanthia . . . *you*
Were healthy, *you* were beautiful. When you died
I stopped writing plays myself, and became a doctor. . . .
Oh, well . . . things long ago! Come, pleasant dog,
Now shall we make the paths of Greece our friends.

*(*AESCULAPIUS *and the* DOG *go off.* ACTORS *continue rehearsing lines.)*

SECOND ACTOR
This hand has choked the one who gave me life—I smelled her
dying . . .

FIRST ACTOR
He slaughtered his own child—and mine—our daughter,
To calm the Thracian winds—

THIRD ACTOR *(as* ORESTES, *looking back behind him and seeing the* FURIES*)*
You can't see them, but *I* see them. They are after me! I can't stay
a moment more!

(The THIRD ACTOR *runs off screaming. The* FIFTH ACTOR *enters, attired as* OEDIPUS, *blinded, with blood streaming from his eye sockets.)*

FIFTH ACTOR
    Apollo did not do this.

The Great Ball

(Chinese music. It is dusk. Two Chinese travelers, SUNG *and* WO, *and one American,* JESPERSON, *are in the mountains on a long journey home. They come upon a place where many people are dancing around a huge china ball.)*

SUNG

The Great Ball of China!

(He tries to budge it.)

Ooof! Impossible to lift it! Even to roll it!

JESPERSON

Who built this ball, or is it a social event?

WO

The common people of China. It is one—and both.

(Very dark and cool Chinese night.)

The Boat from Mandraki

(Just off the coast of the island of Hydra, in Greece. Members of a Greek family are in a small boat, trying to get it to start.)

KAPOS
I'm trying to get the boat started.

TAPOS
It just won't start.

*(*KAPOS *pulls hard and the* MOTOR *makes a sound.)*

MOTOR
Brrrrrrrr whmmmmmmmmmp

KAPOS
Ah, here it comes.

MOTOR *(dying)*
Pzzzzzzzzzzz

BAPOS
No, there it goes.

MOTOR
Kag kag kag kag kag

KAPOS
It goes

MOTOR
Zzzzzzzz

BAPOS
And then it doesn't go.

KAPOS
The sea is becalmed.

ELENA
The boat won't start.

DIVOKOPOULOS
> The Aegean trade was always a risky affair!

MOTOR
> Kagaga kagag brr brr vadoom pttttt pttt zeeeeeeee

KAPOS
> But now it starts, it goes!
> Oh thank you, Kathalassa, Goddess of Boat Parts!
> Kalispéra sas, kaliníchta, efcharistó!

ALL
> Thank you. Efcharistó!

ZAPOS
> Why must we be always in our boat?

KAPOS
> We come from islands
> That have no farmable land. We are doomed to roam the earth.
> We must always be on the sea,
> Trading. We trade for the Doge and for the Turkish Emir.
> If only we had land!

MOTOR
> Shkrrrrrr Shkrrrrrrr Ktiktiki kling zting

BAPOS
> The boat has stopped again. There's something wrong
> Terribly wrong with this whole economy of Greece!

MOTOR *(dying definitively)*
> Fzzz Fzzz zzzz zz.

The Choice in Shanghai

CHORUS
    The construction of the Peace Hotel
    Is almost finished!
    It has enormous rooms!
    Look at it: Here beside the wavering
    Turgidesque-rapid waters of the River, Huang-Po
    "I love you so," inside says
    Ho Kai the Chinese house painter.

(Pause. HO KAI appears at the top of the stairs and begins walking down.)

    Now he walks down the stairs
    Of newly completed hotel
    And "Ah-ooh," he says and we let him say
    For he's so happy
    Feeling at the center of China
    Which, for him, is of the world—
    Out through the lobby and into the street.

(HO KAI, now on the curb of the street, speaks with exhilaration.)

HO KAI
    It is today that I love you!

(HO KAI walks into the street, and a car hits him.)

CHORUS
    Someone, or something, from this encounter
    Has to be wrecked, or to die.
    Show by your applause, which do you choose—the car or Ho Kai?

(The CHORUS *points to* HO KAI *and the* CAR *in turn. While the audience is trying to decide, a* WHITE BEAR *comes in, pushes the* CHORUS *aside, and picks up* HO KAI *in his arms.)*

WHITE BEAR
    I choose Ho Kai.

(Applause.)

Dumplings

(A Shanghai food shop. Everything happens very fast.)

PING HU *(holding up a dumpling)*
    The first dumpling!
    What is a dumpling?
    You shall see, how here it is, actually in fact for the first time
    In all eternity being made by me, the dumpling!
    May god be praised for dumpling
    Which gives up sides and center, top and bottom, meat to enter,
    We to eat it, stunning fruit,
    A man-made woman-made delicacy, the blessed taste-tingling
        ardency of the world.

(DON CHING HOY enters.)

DON CHING
    I am Don Ching Hoy and I demand the first dumpling.

PING HU *(giving DON CHING a dumpling)*
    From this day, dumplings shall be named for you:
    Ching Hoy dumplings—and Ching Hoy means dumplings.

DON CHING
    And what about you who made it?

PING HU
    Many are the ways of being great.
    Another dumpling shall be named after me
    And call Ping Hu.
    The two dumplings!

BOTH
    To the two dumplings!
    To you! To you! *(to audience)* To you!

(Enter a child, a little girl, DANG JOY.)

DANG JOY
> And Tu Yu shall be the third dumpling!

ALL
> Yes, hurray! One two and three dumplings—
> Ching Hoy, Ping Hu, and Tu Yu.
> And this little girl who thought of this game,
> This way of naming the third dumpling?

DANG JOY
> My am Dang Joy.

DON CHING *and* PING HU
> Let a fourth dumpling be named
> And its name be Dang Joy!

(Explosions, music, and very hot day. Dancing in the streets.)

Alexander

ALEXANDER *(moving through an abstract space)*
>When I lived in the clouds
>I was not called Alexander
>But "The Dog." Men looked
>Up at the sky and saw the Dog Star.
>In poetry, I became a line;
>In nature, an umbelliferous plant,
>Smyrnium Olusatrum.
>
>Everywhere the day became Alexander.
>Sometimes I found myself looking at the green
>And gray of a Thessalian morning and thinking,
>Even saying, This is Alexander, I.
>Later those days the blue sky
>Seemed immutable Alexander.
>What is there left to me now?

SAGE
>I don't know, Alexander. Alexander, cinnamon tree.

Olive Oyl Commandeers Popeye's Gunboat and Sails Off to Attack Russia

(A gunboat. The actors speak the lines from behind big stationary cut-out cardboard or wooden figures of OLIVE OYL *and* WIMPY.*)*

OLIVE

    Okay, Wimpy! Hand over those controls! This barge is going to
        Russia. We're going to blow those bastards up!

WIMPY

    Olive Oyl! What? Have you gone crazy? What will Popeye say? He
        is a man of peace.

OLIVE

    Well, he has peace now. If you go down belowdecks
    You'll find him, strangled, and with a knife in his belly—
    A perfect "statue" of peace. He put my child in his tomb!

WIMPY

    Olive—no!

OLIVE

    You too must die, Wimpy! For America!
    And for the good of the democratic world! Now, OFF
    To Russia!

(The boat veers about and a large, menacing face of OLIVE OYL *fills the whole stage.)*

After the Return of the Avant-Garde

(Large city square. MAN *and* WOMAN *standing near a door.)*

WOMAN
>They said of the Avant-Garde
>That it had no lasting power
>But now it has come back
>And everything is changed!

MAN
>Yes, look!
>The door has changed
>Through which we used to walk!

WOMAN
>It is no longer a door now—
>It is a mosque!

*(*ARABS *come out of the door, playing saxophones.)*

MAN DRIVING PAST IN A CAR
>What do you think is the most beautiful thing
>In the Avant-Garde city?

WOMAN AT A WINDOW
>Any three buildings taken alone.

MAN COMING DOWN IN A PARACHUTE
>What about the whole of the Avant-Garde city?

PERSON WITH FEET STICKING UP OUT OF A MANHOLE
>That, too, is beautiful, but in a different way.

(Night falls. Darkness. ANNOUNCER *speaks from high on a roof with a search-light:)*

ANNOUNCER
>Which is more avant-garde—a giraffe or an elephant?

RESPONDENT *(from below)*
A giraffe is more avant-garde, but an elephant is more surreal.

(Music.)

Les Bousculades de l'Amour, suivies de The Mexicana

(A place in the Caribbean. Misty. In the distance one can see a crowd of people. Nearby are EDWARD *and* CHRISTINE.*)*

CHRISTINE

The mood of this island is being distracted
By these four hundred people
Who have come here from the bumps.

EDWARD

What are the bumps . . . Christine?

CHRISTINE

Oh! You called me by my name. Tell me
That at other times we can talk of other things.
But now the hot night, the mercurial pacings of the dancers
And the sea tanager's wild cry distract my heart.

EDWARD

Christine you talk like the Omniplex Literary Encyclopedia
But you do it without art. Kiss me. Now, what are the bumps?

(The scene changes, or it may be just that the people in the distance become clearer. In any case, the scene is many Mexican people in a soft summer evening light. They are dancing gently in a big yard or field.)

EDWARD

They're dancing the "Mexicana"

CHRISTINE

Quietly, slightly moving their feet

EDWARD

As if with butterflies' attentiveness

CHRISTINE

And sometimes holding hands.

EDWARD
> From this modest swinging

CHRISTINE
> Come the horror of Inquisition, the blood-slash of a destructive
> nobility, the steamy crash

EDWARD
> Of a seed time of ethical values, the Putsch

CHRISTINE
> And the remorque of brains—from this Mexicana

EDWARD
> Slightly delightfully beginning, almost like a tree gently budding,
> beneath the light spring rain.

The Yangtse

(The stage represents the entire length of the Yangtse River, or at least both ends of it.)

KI FO *(a young man)*
    A branch falls into the Yangtse.

TI FAI *(a young woman)*
    The water pushes it on. And here at the end
    It washes onto the bank.
    It is wet, and there is a white blossom
    On this one tip of it.

KI FO
    Now I shall head for home.

TI FAI
    I will take this branch in my hand.

OLD WOMAN
    However, no one can move
    Because the King has all the stage directions.

OLD MAN
    Then how did the branch move? and the Yangtse River?

(JAI FU appears.)

JAI FU
    It is only the people who are controlled.

Athens Extended Place

(A very large view of Athens and its environs. The stage, as much as possible, should seem like a relief map of the whole area. The first three speeches are spoken by WORKERS *in the outer parts of such a map.)*

VINEYARD WORKER
I am in a vineyard.

DOCKWORKER
I undock the ship.

FIELDHAND
I am a harvester of grain.

PUBLIC CRIER *(in central Athens, at the Pnyx)*
And I am a Public Crier.
It is time now for an election; I send up a signal
Here from the Pnyx, to convene an Assembly of the People.

(He sends up a smoke signal, and the WORKERS *go toward the center of Athens.)*

VINEYARD WORKER
We all come
To the Acropolis.

FIELDHAND
Even though we live where we live—
And it may be rather far—
We are all Athenians.

VINEYARD WORKER
Athens has no city limits.

DOCKWORKER
"City limits"
Is not a conception of ours.

PUBLIC CRIER
No, there isn't for this big city,
Big in the sense it's an extended city,

There isn't a physical end to it, no line
No definite material barrier at all,
There is no circumventory wall.

(The WORKERS, *along with many other citizens, arrive and keep arriving, at
the Pnyx.)*

Beijing Opera League

(Chinese music. The play is in the grandest, brightest, noisiest style of Beijing Opera.)

KING
>Very great King
>Now play baseball
>First and second base.

JAI FU
>Oh Celestial Majesty
>Only one position
>One man can play.

KING
>You teach me a lesson.
>You are new Commander
>Of Royal Army in Cha-Ing.

JAI FU
>Thank you, Celestial Majesty.

(JAI FU goes.)

KING
>Now he is gone
>I will play first
>And second at same time.

(Dance representation of this, with much leg-lifting and turning slowly, etc.)

>Cannot be done.
>Call back Jai Fu
>To rule my kingdom.

(JAI FU returns. He is surrounded by fan-waving beauties, who sing.)

Of all palace ladies
He can choose one—

(laughing)

Or maybe two.

(Cymbals, gongs, incense, bowings, and all depart.)

Byron in Italy

SCENE I. BYRON *is at his desk, writing.* TERESA GUICCIOLI *stands at the opened door.*

BYRON *(composing)*
 So we'll go no more a-roving—

TERESA
 Lord Byron—

BYRON *(still writing)*
 By the light of the moon—

TERESA
 Can I speak to you for a moment?

BYRON
 I'm writing.

TERESA
 Just one word?

BYRON *(making a last effort)*
 So we'll go no more a-roving—

(giving up, but mild and confident)

 Well,
 I think I'll have the knack for it again tomorrow.

(Berlioz-like music.)

SCENE 2. BYRON *is in his bathtub.* TERESA *stands outside the closed bathroom door. Outside the bathroom window one sees the Grand Canal.*

BYRON
 No more a-roving

TERESA
 Byron, Lord Byron—

BYRON

Teresa I'm

TERESA

George Gordon

BYRON

Having a tub

TERESA

Venice is sinking

BYRON

And thinking over

TERESA

Vanishing from sight

BYRON

We'll go no more a-roving

TERESA

Though the night was made for loving

BYRON

Gad, that's it

TERESA

And the day returns too soon

BYRON

Bless you, Teresa

TERESA

It's gone

BYRON

What? What's gone?

TERESA

Venice, Byron, I've been telling you, Venice has vanished from sight.

BYRON

What? What? That's impossible. If there's no Venice, how will I be able to get out of my tub?

(*Now* GONDOLIERS, *in a grand and moving chorus, sing as they sail into view on the Canal.*)

GONDOLIERS
      Though the night was made for loving
      And the day returns too soon
      Yet we'll go no more a-roving
      By the light of the moon!

(On) a Corner (of Nothing) in Africa

EDWARD
>There is absolutely nothing here, you know,
>That you are going to recognize as being
>Parcel of the usual distractions of your time, which, already,
>The bold silence of not being backward commends
>To your own holy
>Idea of yourself as a state
>More than the one that simply drops you here, being
>An effulgence,
>Contrarily and long, of something else.
>As staying here, you stay, if it seems nil absolu
>You are staying, un-apart from the news
>That, its essential shallowness unrelenting,
>Keys its whispers to what might almost promise a fresh
>Wind, that, but for its pure contractions,
>The remedy (elsewhere) is flowering to be.
>Then, as you stick to this being
>Here present, you see that everything is as well
>As not, in the microseconds that they uncloud it
>With rings, to give it back to whatever you have been doing
>That isn't they.

N'MIMBO
>Can you show me that ring, White Man?

EDWARD
>Blond humans.

(N'MIMBO *hands* EDWARD—*and thus covers him with—a river, killing him.*)

N'MIMBO
>Yes, that is one thing you are.

(*Drums.*)

The Coast of West Africa, 1782

(Coast and Atlantic Ocean. On land a big sign or banner announces "KING BEHANZU, THE SHARK.")

BEHANZU

Help me get into these fins
That I may show the Frenchmen my teeth.

SOLDIERS OF BEHANZU'S ARMY

(As they speak, they help BEHANZU *get into a shark costume.)*
We will, Behanzu.
But these Frenchmen are sharp.
They have fire-propelled missiles that break our skins.

BEHANZU

Ah, I will frighten them, strike them,
And eat them.

(By now he is completely disguised as a shark.)

For I am
Behanzu, "The Shark."

(The FRENCH FORCES *land from the sea.* BEHANZU *and his* SOLDIERS *are easily swept aside and knocked down. However, once the* FRENCH FORCES *have gotten a little way past him,* BEHANZU *lifts himself from the ground and begins to speak, in a very loud, commanding voice. At the sound of his voice, his* SOLDIERS *rise also.)*

BEHANZU

To conquer you may try.
I am ready to die.
But know, before you have
Africa, you have to meet The Shark!

(Now the FRENCH FORCES *turn around and do battle with* BEHANZU *and his* SOLDIERS. *The fight is inconclusive. The stage is covered with blood.)*

WITTGENSTEIN
>There are no subjects in the world.

(An ancient cargo ship—circa 1500—arrives in the middle of the stage. WITT-GENSTEIN *gets on the boat, and he waves as it slowly begins to move again, across the stage. He speaks over the railing.)*

>Each subject is a limitation of the world.

(The boat stops. HAMLET *jumps off the boat.)*

HAMLET
>To be, or not to be: that is the question.

*(*MICHELANGELO *enters from one side of the piazza.)*

MICHELANGELO
>The idea, cari maestri, is in the stone!

WITTGENSTEIN, HAMLET, MICHELANGELO *(together)*
>The idea is in the limitation of the not-being stone!

A Tale of Two Cities

(Large public square in the Avant-Garde City.)

CONICAL MAN
>Our avant-garde city is filled with sunlight—
>How beautiful it is!
>No city like this exists in China.

(Enter COOK.*)*

COOK
>No, certainly not!
>In China our city must be very practical—

*(*COOK *dances about in a sort of geometrical pattern, as if to show where things are in the Chinese city.)*

>With restaurant available at every five hundred feet—
>That is why Cook work well and have sure of job.
>As for new touristic hotel
>There are going up
>Even if many thing not function properly
>And so—And so here too you see is lumberyard
>And place to change chalk into fire for cook
>And this to talk
>Back and forth telephone, that hardly work. This
>Is our Chinese city.

CONICAL MAN
>And here is our City of the Avant-Garde.
>Not as practical, of course, in a practical kind of way,
>But intensely enjoyable, and suggestive, you'll see, Cook—
>And I think you'll like in China, before too long,
>Once you have your practicalities, some like this one too.
>Come, I'll show you around.
>Take this Butterfly Mailbox, for instance,
>That gives wishes! And this time-stopping gasoline station

Whose pumps are dreams! Oh, this, and more—
Our windows full of cries of alarm and kisses!
Our sidewalks that explode in thirty flowers
Of blood! All this, oh everything we give to you,
Cook, all that you did not need,
Or did not know you did before!

COOK
Now all is evident!
Avant-Garde will come to China, too,
If I can get it there.
I must go home, start work.
But how to go there?

(She sees a Dada rocket and looks questioningly at CONICAL MAN.*)*

CONICAL MAN
Here, take this Dada rocket, Cook. Good luck. Good-bye!

COOK
Good-bye.

*(*COOK *gets on rocket and flies off.)*

CONICAL MAN
Oh, it's just another day
In the Avant-Garde City,
The only place where such things come to pass—
I'd guess so anyway.
I'm sorry, though, Cook left—
I'd come to like her.

(He walks off, a little sadly, as an avant-garde concert begins in the public square: musique concrète, featuring saws, vacuum cleaners, firetrucks, and breaking glass.)

Down and Out Near the Bay of Naples

(A panoramic view of the Bay of Naples. In the center, just on shore, the SPECK OF FOAM *appears.)*

SPECK OF FOAM
    Out of all being
    I come,
    A tiny speck
    Of white
    Foam—

    Oh!
    You
    Forgot
    Me, and
    I'm
    Gone!

NOBLE

> They say Cortez is coming, at the head of teeming troupes,
> To win all Mexico for his queen, Isabella!
> They say he is in quest of gold, and that he will do or suffer
> anything to get it!

MONTEZUMA

> How is he dressed? What does he look like?

NOBLE

> He is dressed in shining metal and with a feather on his hat.
> He sits astride something with a tail. His skin is white.

MONTEZUMA

> Oh then, oh then, it is he!

NOBLE

> Who?

MONTEZUMA

> Quetzalcoatl, the savior of Tenochtitlán,
> For whom I have waited so long.

(Aztec music and dancing.)

Quetzalcoatl and the Cook

(Mazatlán.)

COOK
> Why do they call you "The Feathered Snake," my Lord?

QUETZALCOATL
> What a sweet, innocent question! Don't you have a Quetzalcoatl in
> China?

COOK
> Maybe. But if we do, we call it by a different name!

(Volcanic explosions.)

The Vanished God

(A rocky, mountainous landscape in Mexico.)

FIRST MAN

> They say Quetzalcoatl was wont to sit down there
> Talking to the Indians, on summer evenings,
> And that they would tell him their secrets, and tell him their
>> dreams;
> Tell him their grievances, too, and ask for his help.
> Quetzalcoatl, though, was unable to help them. He
> Did not have that kind of power.

SECOND MAN

> What became of Quetzalcoatl? For I know that for a long time he
>> has not been here.

FIRST MAN

> He was vanquished, consigned to oblivion by the Christian saints
> Hundreds of years ago. We Indians believe he is hiding in the caves
> Of these mountains, and that he will come back
> And bring us happiness, will release us from the suffering
> That is imposed upon us, day after wretched day.

The Meeting in Mexico

MONTEZUMA
> Well, it's been a good session.
> I hope that you gentlemen are satisfied.

TOMMY TIME
> That seems fine to us. Edward will leave Christine at the train.
> A few years later he will see her and she will be a little older,
> But still ravishing. Never will he forget the soft feel of her hand
> In his, on the Zocalo.

HAPPINESS
> And Cook will be born. That's what really tickles me.
> Cook, actually, up till this time, who hasn't really been in
> > existence.

CORTEZ
> But—let me get it straight. My conquest is assured.

HAPPINESS
> Yes, though I won't be there.

TOMMY TIME
> I, however, will. And what of you, Montezuma?

MONTEZUMA
> I will be remembered in the stone.

(Enter COOK *with* EDWARD, *hundreds of years later.)*

EDWARD
> Oh, Cook, where is Christine?

COOK
> Not born yet, I think.
> Keep walking, though—we may come to her in time.

The Return of Odysseus

PENELOPE
Odyss

ODYSSEUS
I

PENELOPE
That

ODYSSEUS
Penel

PENELOPE
Tapestry

ODYSSEUS
Weaving

PENELOPE
This

ODYSSEUS
No

PENELOPE
Suitors

ODYSSEUS
Dog

PENELOPE
Recognized

ODYSSEUS
Old

PENELOPE
Nurse

ODYSSEUS
It's

PENELOPE
You!

Other Return of Odysseus

(One ACTOR *plays* ODYSSEUS *and* PENELOPE.*)*

Well, Penelope, I'm back. Put on your threadiest dress and let's go forth into the city. I want to show all the suitors what they missed. Oh of course I will! And to show everyone that I'm here. Oh I'm so glad to be back here, Penelope! I should think you would be. Well, I am. Darling Odysseus! Oh, my delight!

The Harbor of Rhodes

(FOUR COLOSSAL FIGURES, each of which stands astride the Harbor of Rhodes. These FIGURES speak loudly and solemnly and their speeches should sound, as much as possible, like the noises one hears in a big harbor. It's most important in this play to give the sense of an enormous, important body of water put to human uses. The FIGURES, to this end, may wish to speak somewhat hollowly; to be unusually deliberate; to have long pauses between words. They may also speak, sometimes, simultaneously.)

FIRST COLOSSAL FIGURE
> Twenty-five thousand tons
> In one day, sitting on the water.

SECOND COLOSSAL FIGURE
> I want water.

THIRD COLOSSAL FIGURE
> Then these ships move on, over the water.

FOURTH COLOSSAL FIGURE
> What did you say you want?

FIRST COLOSSAL FIGURE
> Twenty-five, thirty, forty, fifty thousand tons per day.

SECOND COLOSSAL FIGURE
> Water. Water. I want water.

THIRD COLOSSAL FIGURE
> This is what it possibly is.

FOURTH COLOSSAL FIGURE
> All we have is harbor water. Harbor water.

FIRST COLOSSAL FIGURE
> Each vessel carrying tons and tons
> Of whatever it is.

SECOND COLOSSAL FIGURE
> Maybe that will be all right.

THIRD COLOSSAL FIGURE
    Heavy. So heavy it is. They
    Move it across the water.

FOURTH COLOSSAL FIGURE
    Is it good water?

FIRST COLOSSAL FIGURE
    From one side to another, the tremendous tonnage
    Moves on the surface of the water of our harbor. When it leaves
        our harbor
    I do not know where it goes.

SECOND COLOSSAL FIGURE
    Yes. It is good water.
    Give me some more water.

THIRD COLOSSAL FIGURE
    It goes to another harbor.

FOURTH COLOSSAL FIGURE
    Here. Here it is.

FIRST COLOSSAL FIGURE
    Yes. That is where it goes. Ton after ton

SECOND COLOSSAL FIGURE
    Thank you. It is good water.

THIRD COLOSSAL FIGURE
    After ton after ton
    After ton after ton

FOURTH COLOSSAL FIGURE
    Every day—
    And then to another harbor.

(Real harbor sounds now begin and grow very loud, so that the voices of the COLOSSAL FIGURES *can no longer be heard.)*

Crêpe de Chine

ONE
> Hi! What's happening?

TWO
> Bozo just sold the avant-garde to China!

ONE
> That Bozo!

TWO
> Millions of men and women walk back and forward, chanting, "Bozo! Bozo!"

ONE
> What has that got to do with anything?

TWO
> Well, just come over here and see!

(The two walk to the edge of a tremendous dazzling uproar.)

CHINESE PEOPLE
> China is avant-garde! Long live Bozo!

BOZO
> Aw nuts, folks, it wasn't nothing!

CHINESE PEOPLE
> Bozo for Ruler of the World!

BOZO
> Oh, come on! Oh well, oh well, all right!

Epilogue

GEORGE
> That's the silliest thing I ever heard! Did you write that?

    Yes. It's my new play, *Bozo, King of China.*

GEORGE
    You should be shot!

St. Petersburg in 1793

<hr>

(A very poor, barren, canal-side area near a livestock market, with dirty snow. Huddled together are a number of workmen, CARRIERS, *who transport things into the main part of the city.)*

CARRIERS
> We carriers have a wretched town of our own
> Here beyond the Ligovich Canal.
> It is cut by empty spaces, phew, empty spaces
> That a man has no wish to walk across—
> No nature and no city, emptiness
> Such as in only city empty spaces,
> Beyond the Ligovich Canal—
> While hustly bustly fur-wound brilliant Russian life
> Lights up the Neva's and the Nevska's byways
> We see it from afar or we imagine
> What happens in those rich and crowded spaces.
> We have a livestock market, and that's all.

(Livestock sounds: mooing, neighing, bleating.)

> We have the livestock with us, and that's all.

(The scene changes to central St. Petersburg. People in fur coats, hats, and gloves go quickly through the streets and speak to one another.)

WELL-TO-DO CITIZENS
> Do you know how artificial the city of St. Petersburg is?
> It was built for the Czar by the Czar without any connection to the
> > slightest sort of practicality
> And without any concern for economic reality.
> The Neva is beautiful and the Nevska
> And the Nevsky Prospect in winter is a beautiful sight
> But think of all those people working in the night
> To make this grotesque city what it is
> Contra naturam is what it is

And yet so pretty.
A city is like a big artificial flower.
Some cities grow up naturally
In a naturally hospitable place.
To these cities Happiness comes sometimes,
And they have walls and are sometimes self-sufficient.
Not St. Petersburg. It's far from self-sufficient.
It's entirely dependent on what comes in from outside

(Enter CARRIERS, *transporting things.)*

And on the carriers, who have a miserable life.

A Love Play

(A room. Faint Chinese music and, outside, suggestions of Chinese landscape.)

WOMAN
>Undress me.

MAN
>I can't. We're in China.

WOMAN
>Oh, I forgot.

MAN
>However—

WOMAN
>What?

MAN
>No one in China can see us.

WOMAN
>Well, that's a thought!

Trade

(The Lido of Venice in 1487. Many flat wooden or papier-mâché cattle are brought onstage and set down in varied positions. The stage is almost filled with them. Enter ANTONIO, *the cattle-keeper.)*

ANTONIO
> Here on
> The
> Lido
> We
> Will
> Keep
> The
> Cattle un-
> Til
> Such
> Time
> As
> They
> Are
> Needed
> In
> The
> City, and
> Then we
> Will
> Slaughter
> Them.

CATTLE
> MAW, MAW—MUUH—
> Cattle don't talk
> But at this we balk
> Why should we be slaughtered on
> The Lido white as chalk?

ANTONIO

> Men need to eat you.
> Otherwise they beat you
> With a stick to make you walk.

CATTLE

> All is fiddle-faddle
> Once you're born as cattle
> Nothing works out.

(Enter two GENTLEMEN, *in big, Venetian furs.)*

FIRST GENTLEMAN

> Venice, a mighty mercantile power,
> Has everything—for instance,
> Witness, my lord, this. *(He indicates the cattle.)*

SECOND GENTLEMAN

> I am impressed. All right, you have the order.
> Fifteen thousand sesterces by Thursday next.

CATTLE

> MUH-MAW-MUUH

(The CATTLE *are pushed offstage.)*

Allegory of Sports

(A rice paddy. A straw-hatted Chinese RICE WORKER *is paddling a little boat.
Enter, with his army behind him,* MAO TSE-TUNG, *dressed as a golfer, in a cap
and carrying golf balls. This play should be done with great intensity.)*

RICE WORKER
      You can't play golf
      In a rice paddy. It's natural
      Enough. Some of these kinds of
      Rices have extremely long stems.
      The water can be eight feet deep.

MAO TSE-TUNG
      Nonetheless we have come here
      With our clubs. We
      Want to "play through." Our
      Tournament is called "The Long March."

Mao Tse-tung Comes Back to Life

(In Beijing's main square. MAO TSE-TUNG *rises from the dead and speaks.)*

MAO TSE-TUNG
    Even he who overturns one stone has eliminated the need to
        overturn that one again.
    What we did was right. What we did was wrong. What is certain is
        that we did something.
    China is not the same. Can you imagine that?
    It really has changed. Whether for good or bad, this enormous
        country is different
    From the way it used to be. Bells in the morning and drums in the
        afternoon,
    That has stayed. But we also have factory whistles
    And the buzzing of the New Flaws of Beijing!

(Whistling and buzzing PERSONS *go past on bicycles.)*

    And the happy smiles of those who have enough to eat

JAI FU
    And the unfortunately pained smiles of those you have tortured—

MAO TSE-TUNG
    Who before did not.

JAI FU
    Who deserved it not.

Un Mélange de Styles

(A beautiful, Balanchinesque BALLERINA *comes floating onto the stage.)*

BALLERINA
  The sky—

(Four Kabukiesque KINGS, *à la Ariane Mnouchkine, whirl onstage sighing and shrieking, groaning, intense, violent, wild, full of power.)*

FIRST KING
  Être, ou ne pas être, voici la question!

SECOND KING
  Tâche damnée, soit effacée!

THIRD KING
  Éteindre la lumière, et éteindre la lumière . . .

FOURTH KING
  Harry, tu m'as volé ma jeunesse!

(Empty carts scoot by. KANTOR *enters dressed in black and drops dead. The* PRINCE *from Swan Lake enters Balanchinesquely, and, meaning to embrace the* BALLERINA, *tries instead to take one of the Kabuki* KINGS *in his arms. The* KING *hurls him into the air. Gospel singing bursts forth, enthusiastic and loud, and the play is over.)*

In the Market Economy, or Lost in Finance

EDMUNDSON
>In the market economy
>I wandered around.
>I wasn't exactly lost
>And I wasn't exactly found.
>For all good things
>They wanted silver or gold.
>In the market economy
>I grew cold.
>Some people were born
>Before market economy began.
>Now I am getting older
>And I still don't understand.
>I will go to the Netherlands,
>To Rotterdam and Amsterdam,
>And be in the great ports before I die.

(He goes off.)

The Precious Sea

MARTÍN DE ACUÑA
    Do you think we will be able to tell
    When the Mediterranean region begins?

GUZMÁN DE SILVA
    Yes. Olive trees.

MARTÍN DE ACUÑA
    Do you think we will be able to tell
    When it ends?

GUZMÁN DE SILVA
    Yes. Palms.

MARTÍN DE ACUÑA
    What is the weather of this region?

GUZMÁN DE SILVA
    Cold from the Atlantic, hot from the Sahara.
    Storm from the Atlantic, calm from the Sahara.
    The right mixture is the best of all.

MARTÍN DE ACUÑA
    I think we are getting near it. Aren't those olives?

GUZMÁN DE SILVA
    Yes—they are. . . . And now we are through it.

MARTÍN DE ACUÑA
    Already?

GUZMÁN DE SILVA
    Yes. These are palms.

Mahx Bruddahs

(Two TOUGH GUYS *are walking along.)*

FIRST TOUGH GUY
> I juss see dis fillum, wid de Mahx Bruddahs.

SECOND TOUGH GUY
> Yeh, I tink de guy said dat dey was Jewish.

FIRST TOUGH GUY
> Jewish! Man, dey was funny, dats what dey was.
> Jewish or nuttin, dose guys is really funny, dey make ya laugh.
> I doan keh when I laff nuttin if somebody's Jewish!

SECOND TOUGH GUY
> Yeh, it's de same wit girls ya really go for somebody, shit!
> Who kehs if dey're Catlick or someting or Jewish?

FIRST TOUGH GUY
> Dats de way it is wid me and de Mahx Bruddahs, fuck de Jewish
> I jess laff all movie Ha ha ha ha ha ha!

SECOND TOUGH GUY
> Jeeze I wanna go see dem guys myself!

FIRST TOUGH GUY
> Stay away from dem ya fuggah! Dey're my girl!

SECOND TOUGH GUY
> Wait a minute. You nutsa sumpin? Dey aint no girl!

FIRST TOUGH GUY
> Yeh, I guess you're right. Oh how I wish dey was!

(He sings:)

> If de Mahx Bruddahs was a girl
> I'd spend all my time in de movies
> Lookin, juss lookin at her!

Come on! Let's go get summin' eat
An' I'll try to fuhget
Dem sweetheart-lookin bruddahs!

The Return of Brad Garks

139

BRAD GARKS

    I've come back to find the Cook
    But how can I find her
    Among these millions and millions of men?

(COOK *appears in the immense crowd of marching and milling humans.*)

COOK

    Because Cook is only woman.
    Hello, Blad Garks!
    So many thing have happen to me
    Since last we met
    In Chengde!
    I have met presidents,
    Famous writers, painters,
    Allegorical figures, talking
    Animals, all. But I am still Cook
    For Blad Garks!

BRAD GARKS

    Oh Celestial Universe, cohere!
    And bring Cook to my heart!

COOK

    Our attraction for each other
    Is both in difference and in sameness.

BRAD GARKS

    We shall fly to the Bay of Naples

COOK

    What's that?

BRAD GARKS

    And build an amusement park—

COOK

    What's that?

BRAD GARKS

Oh, Cook! Come to me.

COOK

I can't! I am being swept away by this crowd
To destiny, Blad, not ours
But that of China!

BRAD GARKS

Its destiny. . . . What's that?

CROWD

CHINA! CHINA! CHINA!

VOICE

The story of Brad Garks and Cook, who first met in Chengde!

Vuillard

(Édouard VUILLARD, *about seventy years old, is in his house.)*

VUILLARD

In this house I, Édouard Vuillard, have been sitting for nigh on to seventy years, painting interiors as if they were the great, wild, glorious world of outside nature itself. Now I am going to go outside and paint hills, plains, valleys, trees, stones, and clouds as if they were walls and chairs. So all will be outside and inside, both dwelling and strange. Who knows what great new worlds may come of this? Oh, wish me well!

(He walks out into a scene of bewildering beauty—of lamps, tables, chairs, curtains, rugs, paintings, windows—while trees, grass, and sky begin to fill up his house.)

Gnossos

(A public place in ancient Gnossos.)

THE PEOPLE OF GNOSSOS
> Oh muscles! Oh mosses!
> What times we have at Gnossos!
>
> There are the fadings
> Of ancient suns
>
> There are bull baitings, bull leapings, bull acrobatics
> In Gnossos
> Gnossos
> Gnossos the only one
> Yes Gnossos is the only one
>
> There was a place
> Called Gnossos
> And now we are at that time in that place—Gnossos!
> Oh heavenly Gnossos, grant my prayer!
> Let my deer become a bear!
> Let buds blossom everywhere
> To deck the streets of Gnossos!
>
> Take your bedclothes to the street
> Dance with everyone you meet
> Put roses there—on blanket and on sheet
> And sing the songs of Gnossos!

BULL
> I am a bull and am jumped on here!

PEOPLE OF GNOSSOS
> Oh clear and graceful Gnossos!

Time and the Sea

(A busy, blue, small Mediterranean harbor, with many small craft, sailboats predominantly, moving about, sometimes gently bumping into each other. These may be represented by people holding masts and sails or other boat-like things, or by actual boats. TOMMY TIME *enters and gestures toward the boats, which stop moving.)*

TOMMY TIME
>The Mediterranean—I am going to take care of it.

(The scene changes to the Congo River in West Africa. The rather rapidly moving water is crowded with big, lily-like flowers with their stems and leaves and also with Congo residents paddling their pirogues. TOMMY TIME *appears through the thick foliage close to the riverbank. As above, he gestures and everything stops.)*

TOMMY TIME
>The Congo—I am going to keep it moving.

(The scene changes to the Arctic Ocean. Ice floes, walruses, and polar bears float or roam about. Through a snow hedge TOMMY TIME *appears and stops all movement with a gesture.)*

TOMMY TIME
>The Arctic Ocean—it is going to be secure in Time.

KUNG HO *(a Chinese scholar-historian)*
>Why is Time so interested in bodies of water?

HALICAFARNIENSIS *(a Byzantine sage)*
>I don't know. I know only that he is often compared to them—as when men say Time is a river, or Time is like the sea.

Glory, or The Anthology

(In a Parnassian environment, poets' names are called by a MUSE-like personage who may be also TEACHER or ANTHOLOGIST, in any case, clearly the one who determines earthly glory. As each poet's name is called, he or she may appear atop a misty hill, then walk down to join the other poets, who may be writing, drinking, conversing—such a heavenly company as might appear in a work of Poussin or of Titian.)

TEACHER, MUSE, *or* ANTHOLOGIST
  Guido Gozzano.

GOZZANO
  Presente.

TEACHER
  Sergio Corazzini.

CORAZZINI
  Presente.

TEACHER
  Marino Moretti.

MORETTI
  Presente.

TEACHER
  Fausto Martini.

MARTINI
  Presente.

TEACHER
  Sibilla Aleramo.

ALERAMO
  Presente.

TEACHER
  Corrado Govoni.

GOVONI
> Presente.

TEACHER
> Ardengo Soffici.

SOFFICI
> Presente.

TEACHER
> Giovanni Papini.

PAPINI
> Presente.

TEACHER
> Camillo Sbarbaro.

SBARBARO
> Presente.

TEACHER
> Luigi Bartolini.

BARTOLINI
> Presente.

TEACHER
> Giorgio Vigolo.

VIGOLO
> Presente.

TEACHER
> Adriano Grande.

GRANDE
> Presente.

TEACHER
> Carlo Betocchi.

BETOCCHI
> Presente.

TEACHER

Alfonso Gatto.

GATTO

Presente.

TEACHER

Leonardo Sinisgalli.

SINISGALLI

Presente.

TEACHER

Sandro Penna.

PENNA

Presente.

TEACHER, MUSE, *or* ANTHOLOGIST

Poets of Italy—now, and till the End of Time.

(Lightning and thunder.)

Ages

JO
> In China everybody has two ages, a lunar age and a solar age.

FREDDY
> Does that mean you are one age in the daytime and another age at
> night?

(Fireworks.)

JO
> Yes, in the daytime Ho Lin is fifty-three years old.
> At night he is seventy-nine.

FREDDY
> What about Ha Chua, the little girl?

JO
> Ha Chua is eight years old in the morning,
> Ten at noon, eleven in the afternoon,
> And at night she is an incipient beauty of twelve.
> Ho ha, ho ha—

(Fireworks.)

> In China, everyone has first and second age!

(Celebration.)

El Nacimiento de Federico García Lorca in Seville

(The white, sun-emblazoned streets of Seville.)

MEN OF SEVILLE *(offstage)*
In Seville,
In Seville

WOMEN OF SEVILLE *(also offstage)*
Lorca is born.
Look at Baby Lorca.

(BABY LORCA toddles onstage, falls down, frowns, laughs, gets back up, and speaks.)

BABY LORCA
At exactly five o'clock in the afternoon—

MEN *and* WOMEN OF SEVILLE *(offstage)*
Oh, already he's starting to talk in verse!

(Now many HORSES—in fact, men and women in old-fashioned theatrical horse costumes—come out to chat with one another in the streets. Their encounters with one another are mild, affable, friendly, as at the hour of the paseo. What is unlike usual conversations, however, is that what everyone—every horse—is saying is a line, or lines, from Lorca's poetry. Each character may choose his own lines and may repeat the same line or lines over and over or go on to new ones. The lines should be spoken softly and firmly, and all the horses should be speaking them at once.)

The Composition of *Louise*

(A chorus singing the Louise *aria "O Jolie/Soeur choisie" is heard in the distance. The singing comes nearer as the play goes on.)*

ANTROPOS
I hear that Charpentier is writing *Louise*.

LE COMTE DE GREUZES
Where did you hear this? How?

ANTROPOS
From Love itself!

*(*EROS *appears, in all his splendor.)*

EROS
Yes, it was I who said it. It is true.

(The CHORUS *now comes onstage, singing loud and clear.)*

The Taps

(CITIZENS *come tap-dancing down the street, behaving in uncontrolled, wild, and lawless ways.)*

CITIZENS
>Tap tap, tap-tap-tap-tap
>Tap tap, tap-tap-tap-tap

DIONYSIOS *(looking at them with great disapproval)*
>Oof! What a state the world is in—look at them!
>What we need is a Poet
>Whose works are full of good, old-fashioned wisdom,
>Someone to teach them how to live and act. The best are dead,
>>though—
>We'll have to go to Hell to get one back.

XANTHIOS
>How will we get there?

(Enter, with a CORPSE, *a tap-dancing funeral procession.)*

FUNERAL PROCESSION
>Tap tap-tap-tap, tap-tap tap-tap
>Tap tap-tap-tap, tap-tap, tap-tap

DIONYSIOS
>We'll follow that corpse. I'm sure he's headed there.

(They tap-dance after the PROCESSION. *The scene changes to Hades. It's very dark.)*

DIONYSIOS *(to* DIS, *God of the Underworld)*
>O God of this Great Place,
>We need a Poet, and all the best are here.

DIS
>Take any one you like. They're not much good here—always
>>reciting.

(calling) Poets! Eliot! Stevens! Yeats!
There's someone here to see you.

(The POETS *appear.)*

DIONYSIOS
I want to take one of you back to earth.
But how to decide? Which one? Why don't you each recite
One or two of your verses, and I'll choose.

(Each POET *in turn mounts a little podium and recites.)*

YEATS
I have coom all this distance, lookin for faeryland.

ELIOT
I sometimes wonder if that is what Krishna meant
Among other things—or one way of putting the same thing—

STEVENS
Chieftain Iffucan of Azcan in caftan
Of tan with henna hackles, halt!

DIONYSIOS
By God! I'll take all three!

DIS
Good journey back!

*(*DIONYSIOS, XANTHIOS, YEATS, ELIOT, *and* STEVENS *climb up out of Hades toward the Earth. At last, a little light begins to show.)*

DIONYSIOS
Come, Poets, into the day!

(Faint, and then louder and louder sounds of tap-dancing, as CITIZENS *approach to hear them.)*

The Four Atlantics

WOMAN

>There are four Emilies: the Emily of her parents;
>The Emily of her childhood friends, who were many;
>The Emily of her husband, William; and the Emily of her
>children—
>Rick, her son, and Laura, her daughter.

YOUNG MAN

>There are four suns: the sun of the tropics—of the Caribbean
>tropical zones, of Africa, etcetera;
>The sun of the temperate countries; the sun of the North;
>And the sun of the Planets, which holds the system together.

YOUNG WOMAN

>There are four musics: the heard, the unheard, the composed and
>the as yet uncomposed.

MAN

>*(speaking with mounting intensity and excitement, as he indicates each of
>the Atlantics on a large wall map.)*
>And there are four Atlantics:
>The transversal Atlantic of England and France;
>The Atlantic that ends in Santiago de Chile, of Spain;
>Portugal's Atlantic, which begins at the Cape of Good Hope and
>ends at the Azores;
>And the Atlantic of the Middle Ages,
>And even of Classical times, the narrow winding corridor
>That goes from the Strait of Gibraltar to Britain's northmost edge.

The Lost Moment

CHORUS OF MOTHERS WITH INFANTS IN THEIR ARMS
> Babies grow up to be beautiful and passionate women
> And handsome and passionate men.

CHRISTINE
> Why didn't you wait for me at the hotel?

EDWARD
> I don't know. Fear, perhaps.

CHORUS OF MOTHERS
> Babies become variable individuals, lead complex lives,
> Are prey to contending instincts, and are often deflected by
> > outside things.

CHRISTINE
> I stayed there for an hour.

EDWARD
> I'm sorry. I was there. You were late. You didn't come. I went out.
> It was stupid and useless. I tried to come back. But I was blocked
> > by a million cars.

Transposition—Bell to Europe, from China

(A smoky, antique scene in China. Gongs sound. A PRIEST *takes a gong and gives it to the* CONNECTOR, *who, amid smoke, incense, and gongs, departs. A long time passes.)*

CONNECTOR—*in this case,* BELL CARRIER
    How slowly things come about. . . . This bell, for example,
    Which we have been using in China for hundreds and hundreds of
        years,
    Is taking what seems to be forever to carry to the West.
    Far easier to lift
    A bell to a tower than to get someone to accept it
    Whose culture has no use for it. Oh well, the time will come. . . .

*(*CENTURIES *go by, in their characteristic costumes.)*

BELL CARRIER
    Here, what about this bell?

PRIEST
    We have no time for such things here,
    Ding-dong, Chinese, and frivolous.

YOUNG DUCHESS
    Why, what would we do with a bell?
    He seems a sweet old fellow—but, a bell . . .
    What sort of accompaniment to our Dark-Age songs
    Would that bell be?

LATER PRIEST
    We call our folk to Mass by moderate means and need no bell.
    By inner need and known they come to us
    And heaven, escape from hell.

CHILD
    Oh, I like this bell.

YOUNG ELEVENTH-CENTURY PRIEST
>Brothers, come see this bell.
>Think what a thing it could be, hung above
>Our Lady's shrine, its steep stone chapels, there.
>And it would call the faithful of the flock
>And have a sound divine. Tell me, old man, how can this bell be
>>mine?

BELL CARRIER
>Take it. It is yours.
>Twenty-three hundred years I've carried it
>Waiting till in the West you'd have a use
>For such a thing. More than two thousand years.

(He goes off, and church bells begin to ring all over Europe.)

À la Banque de France

EDMUNDSON
>Hello. I have these letters of credit
>From the Agence Havas.

BANK OFFICIAL
>Aren't you . . . could you be . . . Edmundson?

EDMUNDSON
>Yes, I am he—Count Leo von Edmundson—at your service.

BANK OFFICIAL *(examines the letters of credit)*
>These seem to me to be firmly backed up by cowries
>As well as by silver and gold. Edmundson, you have at last achieved
>Total economic prosperity and financial solidity. My congratulations!
>My most sincere felicitations! You have triumphed in the end.

(Music.)

The Duke of Wellington's Nose

NOSE

> As the nose of the Duke of Wellington
> I obey the facial proprieties
> Of the lords of the realm.
> But, oh, in my secret fantasies

(Now the NOSE *dances.)*

> I inhale fabulous reeks
> And stenches: pissings, excrement, and the perfumes of brothels.
> Sweat is my secret kick
> And bodily female fluids.
> But as the nose of the Duke I sit up
> Happily on his face as he tells me the news
> Of what has been accomplished so far, and what is left to be done,
> To improve the fate of Britons!

(A piled-high dump cart goes past; the NOSE *sniffs. Then the* DUKE *enters, and the* NOSE *bows and goes to him.)*

In the Storm of Love

CYNTHIA
> Tie me to the bed. Use the rope.

EDWARD
> Oh, I don't want to. It's so sad!

CYNTHIA
> What's so sad?

EDWARD
> That things aren't simple, that we're not as simple
> As we used to be, or used to think we'd be—
> And sad, too, that tying you with this rope
> Will only give a momentary pleasure.

CYNTHIA
> Well, that seems quite good to me.

EDWARD
> But—you are a rose.

CYNTHIA
> Then tie me to this fence, and be a bee!

Cook Comes Home

(COOK *is walking in the streets of Chengde, accompanied by a* SECURITY GUARD.)

COOK
>I have come back to find whatever has been left out
>On these Chengde streets. Member of Party
>Force, for security reason now, now I have travel so much,
>Force to accompany me. No reason. I go on old street
>Where first Cook I was and carrying giant tureen
>For wear white cap and cook dress to be seen.
>Allaways to wear white, cap to keep off hair,
>White dress to show stain or spot of food when there.
>I am in different world from Jai Fu trickster
>He who emprisons King with stage directions
>And say no play two base at same time
>His face comes onto screen
>My memory as if in old play I have see him.

(JAI FU *appears.*)

>Jai Fu, where have you been?

JAI FU
>I have been walking, Cook,
>All over China to look for how can city be separate from
>Country you go on train by feet it is always same
>City to country country to city of name
>And with sky of monument. Tired I sleep in park same
>As bum poor undifferentiate person, though I am
>Jai Fu enormous fame. But it is right that it is so, Cook—New
>>China is new game.

COOK
>Jai Fu we walk together and can discuss much
>How good is writing of some person how of other so pretty is
>>touch

How beauty come and go how some have fame and so
Then none. This all forgotten in game of China.

SECURITY GUARD
Come, you two talking long enough.

COOK
But we don't have to talk to you at all.

JAI FU
Begone! Whoof!

(He makes a magical gesture and the SECURITY GUARD *disappears.)*

COOK
Let us stop in small peasant hut, Jai Fu,
To rest ourselves.

JAI FU
Yes. And to see what time has done
To long-life-clutching, endless-long-touching China.

A Mournful Geography

(Two MEN *are walking across the top of a mountain range.)*

SERGEI PETIKOWSKY

To grasp the enormousness of Russia, you have to see that all the world's populations could fit within its borders. Although, it's true, they would not find enough to eat. And another aspect of its enormity: when, at the height of summer, the daylight lasts, at one end of the country, sixteen hours, at another it lasts twenty-three.

(Blazing light, then normal daylight; then dark, then bright, then normal again.)

IVAN VESTOV

Did Russia, too, like enormous China, always desire peace? And did it regard itself as the center of the world?

(Gunfire is heard faintly in the distance.)

SERGEI PETIKOWSKY

For some reason, no. At least, I don't think so. The Emperor in Peking thought the world would come to him—if it wasn't already there. The Russians kept looking.

IVAN VESTOV

And where did they finally find the world they wanted?

*(*SERGEI PETIKOWSKY *indicates Siberia with a gesture of his hand. As he does so, snow begins to fall.)*

SERGEI PETIKOWSKY

In Siberia, which they sailed to from the Estuary of the Ob—or came to by overland routes. But—quickly, silence. Here is One who might tell us the truth about these things.

(Enter the GHOST OF PETER THE GREAT.*)*

GHOST

I tried a personal rule. And to end my country's isolation. I had a
great capital built in the middle of nothingness. And nothingness is
what it will all remain.

SERGEI PETIKOWSKY

Don't be distressed, Ghost. Great Ghost. Did Russia, like China,
regard itself as the center and always wish for peace? Was Siberia
"invented" by Russia as America was by Europe?

GHOST

No. Nyet. Farewell.

(GHOST *disappears in the mist, and the snow falls more heavily.*)

City Vanguard

(There is a very bright spotlight shining on the center of the stage. The characters go and stand in this light when they speak. It shines directly on their faces, so that the audience has the impression of being spoken to by bright, blazing visages.)

ANN
> The vote has been taken

ROBERT
> Avant-gardism or no

CATHERINE
> And of this the most serious issue

DAVID
> Is whether cerebralism and dehumanization

EDITH
> Are fundamental to its character—

JANE
> And, if the answer is yes,

FRANK
> How will they, joined

ELOISE
> To arbitrariness and spontaneity

GEORGE
> Affect people and things—

GLORIA
> Is the day less bright if it is made of stone?

(At the end, blazing light whites out everything.)

The Stove of Peace

(Deep in Africa, a clearing in a village. Center-stage is a large earthen stove. M'BAMU *and his sons and daughters keep stuffing things into it; it smokes and smokes.)*

TRAVELER
What is that?

M'BAMU
The Stove of Peace.
In it we burn everything that makes war.

(African dances; the stove continues to be fed.)

The End

(Many CHARACTERS *from preceding plays, along with some* NEW CHARAC-TERS, *come onto a large public square, walk about, and occasionally stop to speak to one another. Toward the end, there is a gradually increasing intensity. This is what the* CHARACTERS *say:)*

All women become like their mothers. This is their tragedy.
No man does. That's his.

I see, perhaps, in this peculiar turning,
An anti-European movement destined to turn into fanaticism
And find expression in the wildest rage—Sir Robert Hart, French
     Consul in Cairo.

Before going on, we need, I believe, to insert a long parenthesis
To examine the unused possibilities of the avant-garde.

What good is a play that doesn't even carry us beyond all plays?

You should be careful how long you look into the abyss,
For the abyss is also looking into you.

After a stop in Manila, American silver also crossed the Pacific
And again ended up in China, by this new route.

Yield and overcome;
Bend and be straight;
Empty and be full;
Wear out and be new;
Have little and gain;
Have much and be confused.

What about the voice inside the logic of the supplement?
Within that which should be called the "graphic" of the
     supplement?

Dixit Lope de Vega, annum sixteen oh seven, in Madrid's
      Golden Age:
"Todo se ha vuelto tiendes"—
Everything has been transformed into shops.

Dark, unconscious Forces shape our lives.

The soul is born old but grows young. That is the comedy of life.
The body is born young and grows old. That is life's tragedy.

This culminates in a brilliant homogeneous group of early Cubist
      paintings
Executed at Horta de San Juan, in Spain,

                              Alongside friends,
Who, limited and in the minority, yet active and powerful,
Are characteristic of modern growth.

Can all this change?

*(A very bright curtain falls; or bright red, orange, pink, green, and yellow light-
beams sweep everyone offstage.)*

E N D

A Note on the Type

The text of this book was set in a film version of Ehrhardt,
a type face receiving its name from the Ehrhardt foundry
in Frankfurt. The original design of the face was the work
of Nicholas Kis, a Hungarian punch cutter known to have
worked in Amsterdam from 1680 to 1689. The modern
version of Ehrhardt was cut by The Monotype
Corporation of London in 1937.

Composed by Graphic Composition, Inc., Athens, Georgia
Printed and bound by Fairfield Graphics,
Fairfield, Pennsylvania
Designed by Harry Ford